TAKE THE GUESSWORK OUT OF FINDING AND BEDDING THE ONE YOU WANT TO LOVE...

Whether you like your playmates tall or short, strong or supple, aggressive or passive, straightforward or kinky, this ultimate guide to the pursuit of sensuous happiness clearly and candidly reveals the most intimate truths about men and women of every sign of the zodiac. With this marvelous new handbook, *definitely not for prudes*, you won't have to ask—just enjoy, enjoy!

MARLOWE and URNA GRAY are two handsome and sensuous people who also happen to be well-known astrologers and psychics, especially noted for their public performances of their extraordinary talents.

More Books from SIGNET That You Will Enjoy

☐ **AN ABZ OF LOVE by Inge and Sten Hegeler.** A Connoisseur Guide to Lovemaking more revealing than **The Joy of Sex**, presenting the fine art of lovemaking in words and pictures that describe, with complete candor, all the many deliciously stimulating things a couple can do with each other to make their sex life richer and more varied. (#W5872—$1.50)

☐ **THE SENSUOUS PERSON by Dr. Albert Ellis.** Everybody loves a lover and everybody is trying to become one by reading all those conflicting sex books. Now at last Dr. Albert Ellis, pioneer sexologist, has written a book to give you some honest answers about true sensuousness. He puts in what all the others left out! (#W5735—$1.50)

☐ **THE SEXUALLY FULFILLED WOMAN: A Step-by-Step Guide to the Power of Positive Sex for Women by Rachel Copelan.** Unless you are that rare one woman in ten who has never had any sexual difficulty, this book has been written for you. By following the Seven Steps to Sexual Satisfaction, you too can cure yourself of emotional inhibitions and achieve the ultimate in sexual satisfaction. (#W5676—$1.50)

☐ **THE SEXUALLY FULFILLED MAN: A Step-by-Step Guide to the Power of Positive Sex for Men by Rachel Copelan.** The most erotic part of anyone's body is his or her mind. Now Rachel Copelan reveals how through the use of exercise, Creative Meditation and Auto-suggestion you can become a sexually fulfilled man. (#W5675—$1.50)

THE NEW AMERICAN LIBRARY, INC.,
P.O. Box 999, Bergenfield, New Jersey 07621

Please send me the SIGNET BOOKS I have checked above. I am enclosing $_____(check or money order—no currency or C.O.D.'s). Please include the list price plus 25¢ a copy to cover handling and mailing costs. (Prices and numbers are subject to change without notice.)

Name_____

Address_____

City_____ State_____ Zip Code_____

Allow at least 3 weeks for delivery

The Lovers' Guide to SENSUOUS ASTROLOGY

by
Marlowe and Urna Gray

A SIGNET BOOK
NEW AMERICAN LIBRARY
TIMES MIRROR

COPYRIGHT © 1974 BY MARLOWE AND URNA GRAY

All rights reserved

 SIGNET TRADEMARK REG. U.S. PAT. OFF. AND FOREIGN COUNTRIES
REGISTERED TRADEMARK—MARCA REGISTRADA
HECHO EN CHICAGO, U.S.A.

SIGNET, SIGNET CLASSICS, MENTOR, PLUME AND MERIDIAN BOOKS
are published by The New American Library, Inc.,
1301 Avenue of the Americas, New York, New York 10019

FIRST PRINTING, NOVEMBER, 1974

1 2 3 4 5 6 7 8 9

PRINTED IN THE UNITED STATES OF AMERICA

This book is dedicated to you, the reader, for full enjoyment as you find yourself becoming masters of the art of sensuous astrology.

We gratefully acknowledge the assistance of L. John Wachtel and Bob Freund for their efforts in helping us compile this guide.

Contents

Introduction by L. John Wachtel	xi
Rules	xv

THE TWELVE SIGNS

ARIES (*March 21–April 19*)

The Aries Man	1
The Aries Woman	9

TAURUS (*April 20–May 20*)

The Taurus Man	18
The Taurus Woman	27

GEMINI (*May 21–June 21*)

The Gemini Man	35
The Gemini Woman	43

CANCER (*June 22–July 21*)

The Cancer Man	51
The Cancer Woman	59

LEO (*July 22–August 21*)

The Leo Man	68
The Leo Woman	75

VIRGO (*August 22–September 22*)

The Virgo Man	83
The Virgo Woman	90

LIBRA (*September 23–October 22*)

The Libra Man	98
The Libra Woman	104

SCORPIO (*October 23–November 21*)

The Scorpio Man	112
The Scorpio Woman	121

SAGITTARIUS (*November 22– December 21*)

The Sagittarius Man	129
The Sagittarius Woman	137

CAPRICORN (*December 22–January 20*)

The Capricorn Man	146
The Capricorn Woman	155

AQUARIUS (*January 21–February 19*)

The Aquarius Man	163
The Aquarius Woman	172

PISCES (*February 20–March 20*)

The Pisces Man	178
The Pisces Woman	185

Introduction

I met Marlowe and Urna at a gay and exciting party featuring them as the entertainment of the evening. There was a gold-framed sign beneath a large picture of them resting on an Italian rococo carved easel announcing "Marlowe and Urna Gray—Numerological Astrologers—Now Appearing."

The house lights dimmed in the small ballroom, and a spotlight played on the good-looking features of a tall, handsomely attired and bejeweled Marlowe. Beside him, with striking silver hair, slender and exotic in her black caftan adorned with a necklace of huge diamond-encrusted stars, was Urna.

After a short lecture on the origination of numerology and a brief explanation by Marlowe of what they were going to do, the hour began and passed in what seemed like five minutes.

Asking the month and day of birth from those in the audience, they took turns and proceeded to give "readings," or what they explained to me later were "thumbnail sketches" of each person.

Being half-skeptic at the start of their performance, I was amazed and surprised at their expertise. After every short sketch, the "Ohs" and "Ahs" and "How did he know?" and "How did she do it?" astounded me.

We met backstage, where many others were seeking their "readings," having missed the fun in the short hour allotted to Marlowe and Urna. I waited until the crowed thinned and introduced myself. I expressed my interest in their work, and while we chatted, they explained their busy schedule of performances and the demand they were receiving for readings at private gatherings. All in all, they were kept quite busy and on the run.

Our rapport was excellent, and I set up an afternoon date to meet with them in two weeks' time. I did visit, and to my delight, after a thoroughly interesting discussion about psychic phenomena, numerology, and astrology, they mentioned the concept of a book they were writing.

"The Lovers' Guide to Sensuous Astrology" is going to teach

you how to bed whomever you want to bed, faster, more efficiently, and with less trepidation than ever before." Urna Gray pointed the lighted end of her cigarette at me to emphasize her pronouncement. Both she and Marlowe had entwined themselves into the mass of soft giant cushions on their large couch and were endeavoring to explain the manuscript they had been working on.

"The whole bit with astrology books," Marlowe said in his quietly excited voice, "is that they get too involved with the whys and wherefores of astrological logic, rather than in the end results, which I think the reader wants in a direct and nononsense format."

Their book, *The Lovers' Guide to Sensuous Astrology,* bears out his theory.

Marlowe and Urna are beautiful people, both physically and mentally. They aren't exactly hung up on sex, but they don't deny that the sex drive is a most important part of life, and therefore very important to astrological interpretations.

In the ensuing hour I was informed that although based on a unique mixture of astrology, numerology, and both Urna's and Marlowe's innate psychic ability, *The Lovers' Guide to Sensuous Astrology* is a step-by-step guide to sexual fulfillment without involving the reader in all the ramifications of astrological detail.

Urna was quick to point out that due to lost and forgotten knowledge, astrology is at best an inexact science. Knowledge gained through its use must be carefully scrutinized and analyzed in light of various circumstances.

"Always remember," Marlowe half-interrupted, "astrology is not fatalism, nor is it fortune-telling. It's a window to life. . . ." A smile broke across his handsomely boyish face. "Picture a gigantic bed, big enough for a hundred people . . . you can sleep anywhere you like on this bed . . . and this bed is out in an open field with all sorts of things around, like swamps and deserts and cliffs . . . and you can get out of this bed and move around, or you can drive the bed wherever you like (it's got wheels on it) . . . all that is up to you. All astrology is going to tell you is when the sun's going to shine, or if a hurricane is going to hit, or if you should get out and push, or if you should just lie around all day and make love to everything that comes along. . . . Get the idea?"

I nodded unsurely. Noticing I was still a little in the dark, Urna picked up the thread ends.

"By using astrology, we can get an insight into how each

person is going to do their traveling through life, at least in a general way. In *The Lover's Guide to Sensuous Astrology* we've simply applied these astrological principles to the sex drive and outlined how persons, both male and female of each sign, are prone to act and react.

"But remember, when studying this book," Urna continued, "we are dealing with the subject of sexual astrology in a very general manner. Not all facts will apply to all persons. . . . In fact, what we hope to achieve for the reader is a 40- to 60-percent edge over the competition. Consider how much that edge will help you when combined with an already keen sense of intuition."

Taking the attitude of a very sexy schoolmarm, Urna stated some guidelines to bear in mind while reading *The Lovers' Guide to Sensuous Astrology*.

"Before you read any specific facts about signs in this book, study the Rules chapter. When you've finished it once, reread it to make certain you understand everything. Sexual intrigue is a subtle science, and sometimes you have to study every aspect in order to make your way through the camouflage laid out by your target. After you feel you've mastered the rules, pick out one sign and get to know it thoroughly. Then practice and practice and practice until you get the feel of a general composite picture that will form in your head of the particular sign you're studying. When you can recognize that sign four or five times out of ten, you're ready. . . . Have a ball!"

All the while Urna was talking, Marlowe was gently strumming on a mini-harp he keeps prominently displayed in the living room. As Urna finished her explanation, he struck up a Turkish tempo. Spontaneously, Urna rose from the couch and began undulating around the floor doing a very good *shefty telli* (belly dance). I don't believe either one of them noticed me as I slipped out the door. If they did, they didn't let on.

L. JOHN WACHTEL

Rules

1. At the outset, it is irrelevant what sign your target was born under. What is important is that you decide which sign they look like. Even if they are a different sign than they appear to be, they still will have many of the characteristics of their appearance sign. The value factor of the sign they appear to be is thirty percent.

2. Once you've determined your target's appearance sign, make your initial move based entirely on that sign. *Don't* ask a friend about your target's real birth or sun sign, they may be wrong, and you'll be shot down right in the beginning. Make your approach carefully, feeling your way by performing actions and making statements suggested in that sign's chapter. Adjust as you go. No one will be exactly as the sign described.

3. Once you pass the initial phase and you're pretty certain that you're right about the appearance sign, casually swing the conversation around to the subject of astrology and find out what your target's real birth sign is. If it's different from the appearance sign, then add that sign's facts to those you already have and move ahead on the combined information. If it's the same as the appearance sign, then you've zeroed in and now you can proceed, full tilt.

4. The value factor of your target's real sign is seventy percent. From the time you begin till you've got your target bedded, never lose sight of the fact that every person is an individual and will be different from the "typical" sign described in the book. But remember, if you've moved ahead carefully, you'll be right more than fifty percent of the time. ... Go get 'em, tiger!

ARIES (March 21–April 19)

The Aries Man

Recognition

The Aries man's features are very decided. There's nothing vague about his looks or his personality. His face is sharp, with well-marked, bushy eyebrows placed closely together. These unique eyebrows hover over eyes inclined to glint and sparkle like bits of steel. This characteristic gives the Aries man's eyes a look of excitement and inquisitiveness that generally remains even after his initial interest wanes and wanders.

His neck is long, and his ruddy-complexioned face, although broad at the temples, narrows to thin features with a pointed chin. The hair, carrying out those fantastic eyebrows, is of a rough and wiry texture.

Many Arians have a spare body of medium height or slightly above, and rarely accumulate extra weight.

He knows exactly where he's headed, and walks with an even gait and a great deal of poise and grace. Although his feet are quite definitely on the ground, the Arian often has his head in the clouds, weaving dreams as he walks steadily in a different world from those around him. Despite this dichotomy, there's a provocative dynamism about him when he's trying to get an idea across.

It's best not to disagree with this affirmative sort, because they ordinarily have violent tempers, which they lose easily. They radiate assurance and a positive manner. When an Arian is excited, it's quite a show, particularly when he has instigated the moment or is a part of it. They are inclined to gesticulate wildly with their arms, yet there's always a precision about their movements.

Being a pioneer in spirit, the Aries man will readily wear the newest fashions in clothing. Even the more mature men of this sign will dress in new styles, adopting avant-garde materials and shoes long before the younger ones would dare to even experiment. He'll don the smartest shirt, and in business, dress will be slightly way-out.

The Arian wears a long-hair look and is likely to sport a moustache and/or a beard.

He's a real baby when he's sick, and doesn't visit a doctor or dentist nearly often enough, being inclined to put off anything seriously involved with diet or exercise. Dreaming and doing are at opposite poles for the Arian. The realities don't interest him nearly as much as the imaginative aspects of life.

Along with his flair for clothes, his pioneering spirit extends to jewelry, and he sports necklaces, charms, and amulets. The stones he chooses are most often indicative of his birth month. There's a great excitement for the Arian in expressive jewelry. He likes big, bulky watches in gold, mod-style. Fashion trends carry him to eyeglasses of the newest frame design, naturally with pink-tinted lenses for that much-desired rose-colored view of the world around him.

But his taste is good, and he's able to wear almost anything vivid, combining brilliant and subtle hues effectively, with a special feeling for dramatic blacks and whites. However, red and green are his predominant colors. His feeling for the exotic carries over into the scents he prefers, sparkling, startling scents. He really enjoys the odor of heavy colognes, musky, like perfumed autumn leaves burning.

He's definitely a gourmet, always on the quest for something new and different in the culinary field. He enjoys cooking, too, as long as it's not too difficult and time-consuming. Chinese vegetables, bean sprouts, cabbage, lemon and lime juice, and anything of the sweet-and-sour variety really turns this guy on. If you serve him fish, fix it in a novel way. He absolutely *loves* garlic, and almost any vegetable will tempt him, as long as it's creatively prepared. The Arian likes the flavor of rum in cooking, and dotes on sauces made with sour cream and mayonnaise. He's got a true built-in taste for olives, and will panic those around him when he eats grapefruit and orange slices mixed with radishes, onions, and cucumbers.

Strangely, with all this variety, he'll settle happily for ordinary desserts like apple pie à la mode.

Where to Find Him

You'll find your Aries man exercising his knowledge and flair and exploiting it at any kind of scientific show—expositions involving automobiles, boats, or airplanes. He loves to dabble with new equipment. Possessor of a hidden antenna when it comes to mechanical objects, he is quick to claim his superiority in the field, often suggesting, with no false modesty, how much better an already superior item could be. He's the kind who loves to fool with television sets, likes to figure out how your stereo or radio works, and displays logical approach to fixing just about anything around the house.

At a hobby show, you'll generally find him in the hardware area. His interest is caught by chisels and knives, because he's good with his hands and with tools, and can design and build quality furniture. He prefers working with natural products like granite and wood as opposed to modeling in clay, and is a natural for instructing classes in carving or whittling.

A music lover, he's immediately attracted to the new works of modern composers. If a premiere performance of a composition is being played, you can be sure your Arian will be there. This seeking out of the new and adventurous extends all the way to mountain climbing or cave exploration.

If you can adjust to this diverse and progressive man, that's where he is, so go get him!

Primary Move

In approaching this multi-faceted man, you'd better talk about him, what he's done, how much better he's done it, and how superior his way of doing it is to anyone else's you can think of.

The Aries man isn't really that egotistical; he just firmly believes no one else is his match in certain areas. He comes up with splendid ideas, and if you listen and show your interest, you'll be a cinch to join him. Keep up, but never, never take a stride ahead of him.

And don't ever correct him if you feel he's distorting a few facts. It's really not that important to set him straight. This type has *got* to be right.

If you can take it, you'll be in for a treat, because he really keeps you on a roller coaster. He's always dreaming that magnificent dream, building those incredible materials, and striving to make good things happen.

While you're busy dressing for your first date with this man, just remember, he wants to put you in a special place in his heart, high up on a pedestal. When his interest catches fire, you're practically perfection. And you just don't flirt with anyone else when escorted by the Arian ego.

Pre-coitus

Because the Aries man is pioneering, headstrong, and impulsive, he knows what he wants when he wants it. Which is now! Ironically enough, if you're the woman who wants this man, you will have to be both mysterious and obvious. Obvious in the way you dress, always enticing, teasing, promising the revealing of your body's gifts. Wear an exciting nightgown that shows the roundness of your breasts and derriere or allows an enticing flash of your thighs. You might wear several strands of beads that hang suggestively over your breasts, partially covering them yet slipping between and separating them, reminding the Aries man of your body's ready sexual charms. You've got to be crafty and subtle so that he can always feel he's a pioneer. This means that though you're somewhat exposed, you must always keep partially covered. Reveal the blueprint, but don't give away the square footage.

For example, just casually bending over at the waist to pick something up from the floor with your back to him, derriere outlined, each cheek beautifully defined in a clinging jersey material, excites him. He reflects, then is motivated to touch. The sight of your body suggests rooms smelling of incense and reminds him of champagne flowing.

The new braless look, covered to the neck, but the breasts free underneath, is provocative to an Aries man. Think of a cold piece of ice slipping down your back so your nipples will harden and poke like little poles into the bodice. When he sees the extension of your nipples protruding through the material, you've got a guarantee the pioneer is ready to conquer new realms.

Appearing nude or wearing a monokini with this man won't bring positive results. He's the great hunter in unknown lands and thrives on challenge and discovery, so make him feel there's something to discover. He's Christopher Columbus and you're ripe but virgin territory.

Try a perfume with an oily base sparingly applied and used with finesse in private places—in your hair, behind your ears, between your nose and lips, on your eyelids, in the back of your knees, under your breasts. This combines with your own chemistry to entrance his senses. Shiny, clean, well-groomed hair, any length, stimulates the "virgin"-territory picture for him. He wants to believe he's the only one before, now, and forever. Let your vibrant lustiness shine and lure him.

This man likes new ideas, and is enthusiastic and persistent in his sexual needs. Let him think up new ways to reach you, but be pleasing and enticing enough so that he wants to.

Since he's the leader and is always interested in a woman who is involved in life and interested in everything from gourmet cooking to bookkeeping to ballet, here's your chance to be saucy in a subtle way. Build his enthusiasm by suggestive movements of your body. Put on a record and let yourself move into a Greek belly dance. Wear a bracelet or ring with tiny bells that tinkle in a gentle breeze. Hold miniature cymbals on your fingers in each hand and beat a steady rhythm with them as you do your "Little Egypt" number. The haunting, rustling sounds will evoke pictures of the glamorous Far East and the mysteries there to be explored. To top it off, tie a chiffon handkerchief over your face, exposing only the eyes. This will really do it. You don't need any more of a costume; just the few accessories described will be sufficient. Now move, slowly and subtly, in a rotating, undulating motion, letting your hips be a life unto themselves. The decorous, sensuous "grinds" used in a belly dance are far more wanton-looking to an Aries man than hard "bumps." When grinding, keep the quivering of hips under good control, and do it slowly, accelerating your speed to a crescendo only at the end.

Perform before this man without advancing toward him; make him come to you. You don't have to touch him directly to excite him; in fact, during the pre-coital period, hold back from touching this Aries man's penis or any of his erogenous areas; save that for later, when you're in bed. Be artful about your need; don't tell him you want sex. Wait until you've gotten him stirred by the idea of discovering you, and he'll let you know that he's ready. He doesn't like to be led or told what to do. He's the head of the safari, so let him lead you through the lush jungle of love.

Coitus

In bed, your Aries lover will be patient, gentle, and yielding if things are going smoothly. He is constructive, methodical, and deliberate in his lovemaking. Switch from being mysterious and subtle to being sweet and tender. Let him help you unzip your gown. Hold it protectively for just a fraction of a second over your breasts. Look at him almost shyly as the dress falls while you lift your chest high so your breasts stand out, cherry-nippled, inviting succulent kisses from him. He can't resist. As he bends down to caress your nipples with his tongue, hold his head between your palms, using ever so little pressure as you press his face harder against your longing bosom. He'll get the idea to nuzzle and suck like an infant. Gently pull away and then press your nipples back to his mouth again. You're in third gear now with an Aries man.

He likes sex to go step by step, so it's likely he'll proceed from tender caresses to an exploring sortie of your body. Just like a Ponce de Leon hunting for your fountain of youth, he'll first map his movements out with his fingertips, then follow with a hungry mouth.

Adolescent sex play can be appealing to an Aries man. As his hands define an arc about your perfumed Pandora's box, move your hips just enough so that his fingers can't help but meet that pink, soft, and wet opening, impatient for the lid to be opened. Soon you'll have him remembering his high-school days in the back seat of a car. Memories will make him even more responsive.

Although cunnilingus is usually out of his repetoire, a wet kiss or two at the top of your thigh, close to the crotch, is not too amiss. React, yes; but violently, no! Always smooth movements with girllike exclamations of bliss. Let him feel your legs squirming in pleasure, your calves caressing his.

Now, be more assertive. Handle his body soothingly, moaning quietly with delight. Straddling his chest, start at the temples and massage them gently with two fingers of each hand. If he doesn't have some obsession about his hair, and many Aries men do, let your hands tug at it, increasing the circulation in his scalp. At the same time, let him feel your breasts on his face, the flesh of your inner arm on his cheek. This man likes fluid motion, so don't be jerky in your movements. Don't throw yourself at him with wild animal ardor. Continue your sexual affection by massaging lightly with your fingertips on his face. Move firm hands across his shoulders, his arms, down his hands to his fingertips. When his fingertips are entwined in yours, lift his hands and deftly, warmly kiss the palm. Let your tongue slip in and out between his fingers, using his forefinger like a Popsicle. Dry his hand by running his fingers through your hair. Wet, sticky hands can be an appalling feeling to an Aries man.

Now down the sides of his legs, running your hands over his thigh muscles to the edges of his buttocks. By this time, desire will have reached a peak. He'll lead you to touch his testicles and his penis. He'll put your hand on his testicles and tell you to rub them carefully. As mentioned earlier, puberty-type romance intrigues this man, and his desire may be for you to masturbate his penis. He could possibly cover your hand with his and move your hand at the speed and touch he requires. Your Aries lover is cautious and obstinate, so let him have his way. Let him lead. If you're too aggressive and try to initiate what he doesn't want, you'll only lose him. Remember, in bed follow his orders completely.

He favors the approach from the rear, by placing your body in a fetus position on your side, then entering your vagina from behind, after cuddling in to fit the outline of your body. It is a comfortable way to have sex, and he's in control as to the depth of his thrust and the amount of vigor he chooses to use.

Way-out sex is usually not for him. So, most times, don't expect intricate or involved sexual maneuvers. Simplicity is the word here. Sex is likely to be him on top of you, or you on top of him, so if he places you on top of him, there's every chance you'll be doing all the work.

If you want to be openly, hotly amorous, now's the time; move all you want. Take the great hunter on a trip he'll never forget. Just move in slow circles after mounting him, your legs kneeling on each side of his body as he lies on his back. Sit on his penis while inserting it in your vagina. Then, take his hands in yours, arms upstretched to use as a lever as you rock and roll. Or lie directly on his body, your hips and buttocks riding swiftly and zealously up and down. You needn't be any more inventive than that. Just straight and to the point, honest in your sexual motions.

Your Aries man wants sex regularly and often. He's selfish in his sexual demands, and he will demand. You'll forget all about variations after you've experienced some of that satyrlike energy of his. If you've gotten him enthusiastic and stimulated enough, you'll find he can make love three or four times in session. So rest up and be ready.

Post-coitus

If you're not sexually satisfied, and that's an incredible thought after such a sexual marathon, it would be unwise to tell this man. Never criticize an Aries man regarding his performance in lovemaking; he can't take it. No matter what, be delighted and relaxed. Show him that you are pleased and happy with him. Chances are that your Aries lover will want to hold you and talk to you. He likes to talk and daydream with a woman in his arms, so don't disturb his mood. If you want to get up, make him think it's for him, to make him more comfortable. Bring him his favorite drink, or iced tea if he's a teetotaler, or come back to bed with some fruit. Grapes, perhaps, and feed them to him one by one. The Aries man can be childlike and playful; a little grape and tongue game after sex will please him (and may start things over again!).

Just as in sex, step by step, let him get to know you as a person. Tell him only so much about your greatest desire, then stop. Tease him a little so he'll coax you on. Every time you open another door to yourself, you're offering him the opportunity for more adventure. His needs are frequent, and if you can combine a bright way of speaking to hold his attention, and a great strength and facility in bed—what more could the Aries man want?

By his attitude you'll be able to judge when it's time to straighten the sheets. Wash his body down with a warm washcloth, avoiding sex play, then briskly wipe him dry with a fluffy Turkish towel. Pamper him, but if he wants to get up and go sailing or skiing or walking around the city, be adaptable, you better get up and go too. Follow that leader!

The Aries Women

Recognition

This lady could easily be compared to a Stradivarius violin. She's so tuned up, so tight, so sensitive to every nuance and action, that touching her hand or running a finger up her inner arm causes cold chills up and down her spine. A dynamic sort, the Arian woman loves the outdoors, has vitality and energy to burn. But being human, she runs down occasionally, ignoring the fact that she needs more rest. She's oblivious of the pertinent signs and gives in when she's ready to collapse.

Her face is usually long, atop a slender neck, and her complexion, while a healthy pink, tans beautifully. Her eyes are of average size, but unusual in their look—questioning, wondering. Her mind races quickly, changing images like a kaleidoscope.

She always seems to be in a hurry, never walking if she can run. The Aries lady is optimistic in the extreme, looking forever toward tomorrow, always expecting the sunshine after the rain.

She has full eyebrows, which require attention, like her male zodiac counterpart. You can recognize an Arian female by these eyebrows and by the intense expression on her face, which comes from concentrating so hard and wondering incessantly about everything in life.

Her nose is often long, sometimes with a little dimple at the tip. Her thin lips are suggestive of excitement and dynamism, as opposed to sensuality. The Arian's long, streamlined body seems an extension of her mental liveliness. She has a well-shaped bosom and long, lovely legs that could earn first place in any beauty contest.

Clothes are not the most important item in her life, but she likes the unusual, preferring colors of red, green, and white in most of her wardrobe. She'll affect the African robe, the caftan, loosely hanging but carried like a queen. She'll even wear a sari for fun, but doesn't care for the constriction. When a poncho is acceptable, she'll have one on. She prefers the freedom of well-tailored slacks and blouses, and the ultimate emancipation of the bikini. The Arian woman will jump to dress herself for a sailing venture, because she loves the sport. Of all the signs, she's the one who'll have at least two raincoats and two umbrellas in her closet. She's addicted to walking in the rain. This habit releases her vitality, and plugs her particular cord into a socket, making her feel renewed. This is occasioned by a spring shower or a winter gale, or even a deep snowfall. For the latter, she adores donning warm scarves, sweaters, and all manner of hats—jaunty, saucy, big, little, warm, or foolish.

This girl will respond to a man's after-shave lotion if it's lime-scented, because she favors the fruity odors, the fresh, clean smell of lime, never sweet but not too pungent, either. No flower scents or the exotic aroma of burning incense for the Arian. Her jewelry will be simple and large because she's a big girl. She'll favor an aquamarine in a simple ring setting, or a bloodstone necklace, since it's one of her birthstones. She'll wear it opera length, dangling provocatively between her breasts. She likes the romantic jasper stone, too, and the black onyx captures her imagination. Her ears are usually covered by her hair-do, so she'll affect hanging earrings, usually worn on pierced ears, sticking to the gems she favors. The cost of jewelry is usually inconsequential. However, she adorns herself carefully, making the proper selection important.

This lady generally smokes too much and is often inclined to overindulge in alcohol, faults which mirror her high-wire tension. Moderation is a lifelong battle for her.

The Arian woman is extremely impulsive, enthusiastic, and independent, often taking the lead and becoming aggressive sexually. She likes to be boss, but secretly hopes he'll overwhelm her and assume the reins of leadership. If he does, she's hooked! This lady feels that if she can really string a guy along, it's not worth it, and she loses interest. Somewhere her man must draw the line, say, "Listen to me, girl . . . ." and she will. She's a pushover for flattery, and acknowledges it by purring like a kitten. It's then she can become coquettish and very, very feminine, a state of mind that occurs infrequently with this lady, and only in an exceedingly intimate situation. She's wonderfully adaptable to change. No matter how bad things appear, she's the eternal optimist; her smile is constant and not the least bit phony. When she's disappointed or hurt, that smile pulls her through, and she rarely requires a pep talk to pull her up from the blue depths. A terrible flirt, really, but she doesn't always mean it. She's a tease who'll turn on quickly, and then just as quickly say, "Whoa!" She's much more attracted to a man who's dedicated to his work and interesting pursuits than to the indolent playboy or wolf trying to live off the fat of the land—or anyone else's! She has the capacity to know immediately if a person is involved in life or whether he's just hanging on for the ride, and this latter type she simply cannot abide. If this sort becomes too annoying and insistent, she'll exhibit her fiery temper, because she detests people who are not fulfilling their own potential and living life to the fullest. This outburst may last for an hour, but she doesn't hold grudges.

Where to Find Her

You'll often find the Aries woman in a man's job, because she has zeal and determination plus an enormous vitality. Where you might find a couple of women laborers toiling for "show," you can bet an Arian will be one of them. Nothing ordinary for this gal; she's got to be the president of a company or the chairman of the board. Authority is a *must* with her. She may invade the fashion world because of the constant change and variety it offers, or the ever-challenging field of advertising and promotion. Involvement in life is her thing, so this feeling, combined with her originality of thought, could lead her into women's lib or a liberal political movement. Music's not always high on her list, but if she's involved at all, it will be as a director or a composer, a teacher of theory or the production head of a theatrical company. Acting is generally not her forte. She could be a saleslady, but only if she were breaking in a new product or territory. Selling behind a counter would be absolutely repelling to her. The sameness of each day could drive her mad. The Arian could change jobs more frequently than any other, because once she's got the requisites under control and her work becomes automatic, there's just no more kick in it. She loves change, movement, and challenge.

If she bowls, she'll use all the proper muscles, correct stance, and right techniques. If she studies ballet, it will be for exercise, not performance. She gets a kick out of the mechanical equipment at a gym, but prefers doing it herself. The Arian on a bicycle, look out! She's out to break the speed limit on the freeway. Behind the wheel of a car she's a stock-car racer. She can't help herself; the action and derring-do is part of her inherent makeup.

Primary Move

The sensational, unusual, and odd entertainments are her delight. You could suggest a late supper, then a quickie flight to Las Vegas to break the bank. Or if you're an Easterner, a similar excursion to the Bahamas for a round of blackjack. If you've got the money, you can follow through on this course, but even if you're not loaded, always consider the different, the strange to captivate the Arian woman. Take her to a strip show, or where they feature female impersonators, and she'll be totally immersed. Her mind will rotate like a windmill in a storm, wondering how a lady could shed her clothes in public, or how a guy could turn into such a gorgeous woman. The Arian relishes a clubby, intimate bar with overstuffed chairs or sofas, decorated in red. She'll love an exotic restaurant with, say, a Swedish smorgasbord where the food is colorful and spicy. In fact, when it comes to food, it's got to be tantalizing in the way of flavor and odor and preparation. She adores different specialty dishes from foreign lands, and is very much at home with tomatoes, beets, apples, pimiento, and a hot cocktail sauce with horseradish. She'll go for steamed fish Cantonese style, with chopped onions, spaghetti Milanese, or rumaki as a side dish. All kinds of salads tempt her, from Caesar to antipasto, and she'll find cheese and fruit perfect for dessert. She believes garlic makes one passionate, so don't worry about indulging yourself. She's delightful, and she'll try anything—once.

If you're in Manhattan, treat her to a hansom-cab ride, or if in Altantic City, a chair ride on the boardwalk. If you're a Floridian, a speedboat whirl will have her tuned in strong. Any change of pace is welcome to the Arian female, and once she's convinced you're the one, you've got her. Don't forget, she's aggressive, and she may suggest a visit to your place, for even more variety.

Pre-coitus

If you wanted to hit upon a theme song for the Aries woman, you'd have to choose that old favorite "Falling in Love with Love."

Each romantic interlude in her life is *the* great love affair. It's never just a passing fancy, but love in all its guises. Happy, gay, carefree; heartache, tears, and sorrow. Kisses hello and sad farewells. Glorious mornings, and evenings of despair. Telephones that should ring and don't. Doorbells that are completely silent or alive with chimes. Each and every time *the* new man comes into her life, it's the time of her life. The periods and cycles between men are low, miserable, and uninteresting, but it's her optimistic nature that assures her, "Just around the corner, there's someone waiting for me . . . ." And during the high of the cycle, she'll be overactive, overbusy, overinvolved, and oversexed.

Being around an Aries lass is like watching a soap opera. You know that each moment will bring either some new crisis or pleasure. She does have a headstrong and aggressive way in the romance department. There's no special ideal; it's all in her mind. "Maybe, just maybe . . . that's him. The *man* of my dreams." So, no matter what you look like, you've got a chance. No matter how you think, you could be *him*. The only sure losers in her estimation are playboys and gigolos. She's too experienced and sophisticated in the way of men to find them worthy. The main requisite is that she must feel proud to be with you, for some particular reason or other in her own mind.

Aries women are overly aggressive. If you're on the make, catching you too easily is no challenge to her. Yet, if you play it cool, too hard to get, she'll quickly lose interest. Best way to capture this ephemeral, independent being is to say nice things to her and mean them, but don't make your pass too fast.

A great situation is to invite her on a skiing weekend. A group of your friends, about sixteen in all, are pitching in for a group flight to Aspen, Colorado. Skiing, lodging, cold nights, hot toddies, and a fireplace the size of a room.

Girls assemble together, four in a cabin, men the same. Of course, if you like, you can mention that these boys and girls are mostly good old friends and intimate partners.

A whole portion of the plane is occupied by singing,

happy, healthy-looking people. Joking and laughter abound. Each settee carries two warmly wrapped people, snuggled in their ski sweaters or fur-trimmed parkas, drinking free champagne. As the flight goes on, the champagne no longer flowing, drowsiness comes over the throng. Overhead lights blink out, and whispered conversations replace the hilarity.

You lift the intruding armrest from between the seats and hold her arm, pressing the back of your hand against her breast. As she edges closer, turn your hand around and palm her bosom. Under cover of dark, and really very private in your nook, you can feel her reacting favorably to your touch, moving sideways in her seat, belt undone, her back to the window. She's making it easier to reach beneath her sweater, and you feel the nipple grow hard under your fingertips. She moves her torso forward, anxious for the other breast to be caressed. But clever you manages to reach the second nipple with the same hand, tweaking it and pulling gently on its saucy, upturned peak. Then, rubbing the set back and forth with the palm of your hand, you feel her body trembling in orgasm.

Twenty thousand feet over West Virginia, your ski pants have a built-in Egyptian pyramid. She's quite aware of this welcome intruder and diplomatically covers both your bodies with the wool plaid rug.

Feeling aggressive, and once again in love with love and you, she reaches for the new-fangled buttons that keep you altogether. With her determined nature to get things done right, she manages to free your erection from the close confines of your ski pants. He's so happy to be free, he's doing a male version of the bellydance. And her pleasure is watching every movement with her fingertips.

Strong, hard, and active, he demands her attention, and she acquiesces by burrowing under the afghan to suck him. Psychologically, the conditions under which airy Aries has chosen to satisfy her appetite has made your penis almost an inch longer than usual (at least, it seems so to you), straining to be kissed and pummeled about in her hot mouth.

She's kind of squirming now, wanting and needing your body to herself. Somewhat perplexed, you finally scheme a way to satisfy her. You suggest she jiggle her slacks just over her hips to her knees and cover her body once again up to the waist, sitting close and erect beside you.

Sure she'll find the answer to her twitching, she does exactly as she's told. Sitting down again beside you, she feels your forefinger searching for her lips, then finding the pulsating clitoris. She ensconces herself on your finger, lifts her hips a little; two fingers, once more she lifts; three fingers . . . ah, just right. Somehow the roar of the jet drowns out the ecstatic muffled cries, and she's finding it harder and harder not to bob up and down as you thrust your fingers. Not satisfied being still, she figures if she sits with one leg bent up on the seat and one down, she can move without attracting attention. You have great admiration for her know-how. No wonder she's a successful business girl. That's better. She hopes the plane hits an air pocket so she can dip and dive harder on your vacillating fingers.

This surreptitious fun is interrupted by the stewart's announcement to put out all cigarettes, fasten seat belts, you're ready to descend. Not flustered in the least, your admiration again soars as she deftly undoes your fingers and hand from their unlikely jail, and with one fast jerk unseen by all but you, she adjusts her slacks. Then she's busily chatting about the lights on the landing field looking like jewels, and what a fabulous weekend you're going to have skiing.

Your enthusiasm, as great as hers, makes for a hard, fast kiss, a squeeze of each other's hands, and after several bumpety-bumps you arrive at your destination for love.

Coitus

Bundled in and out of the airport and in and out of the main lodge after registration, you bundle into the cabin for four, which will be occupied by only two. By your special request of the management, the arrangement includes a ghostly third person that never shows up.

After a brief but thorough examination of the quarters you'll be sharing and a plea from Aries to start a fire, she goes into a kitchen the size of a galley. It's stocked with food and whiskey, and she prepares a Scotch sour—orange slices, cherry, and all.

How tranquil and lovely. A fireside, a drink, a cigarette, and the hero of her dreams beside her. And the loveliest touch of all, snow. Curling its feathery way across the window panes, stopping for a moment, then twirling like a ballerina to the great snow mounds below.

With fireglow to compliment her skin tone, she removes the sweater and slacks that interfered with her pleasure. Following a fine example, you do the same, and most willingly.

You approach her now to unsnap the bra and watch two gorgeous breasts bob up, nipples perched like tiny brown sparrows ready to fly . . . into your mouth.

You groan a sound unable to express the fullness of vibrant desire. She understands, and there's an echo from her throat. You laugh together at your obvious mutual agreement. Aries, sensing a serious note, and wanting gaiety and fun in love, playfully plucks the long-stemmed maraschino cherry from the Scotch sour. (A thought crosses your mind like a shadow: "Did she pre-plan this . . . cherry and all? It's supposed to be my party!") It's not necessary to search for an answer to your silent question, because you're too busy watching her performance.

Lying on the sofa in front of the fire, she's opening the lips of her vagina, holding the cherry just at the opening.

She tells you, "Can't you see, I'm a virgin? Come, eat my cherry!"

So she took the play away from you again, who cares? You descend to catch the cherry with your teeth, but succeed in retrieving only the long stem. Ah-ha, better perhaps if you hold it there and nibble easily, letting your tongue flick, lizardlike, into her wet cup. Entranced with your ingenuity in managing the Cherry Chase, she's eager for more, but not of the same.

Mounting your lovely Aries in the "old-fashioned" way, you move in perfect unison until those funny sounds repeat themselves. . . . And for tonight time to sleep curled up in each other's arms.

Post-coitus

Drunkenly staggering from love, not alcohol, arms around each other, you enter the bedroom. Redolent from your long journey and lovemaking, Aries decides a luxurious bath will be just perfection. Three-quarters of an hour later, Aries tiptoes back and finds you lying horizontally on the bed. She maneuvers your body into proper position, your head on the pillow, and cozies down beside you. While you're falling back asleep, disturbed momentarily by her return, you marvel once again at the adaptable, unusual, spontaneous Aries girl.

She whizzes by you on her skies down the medium-steep slope you've chosen to test your own ability and her experience on skis. Once again the Aries girl astounds you. There's just nothing she can't do, and do well. You follow, sure to catch up. Looking ahead, you see she's fallen and is rolling over and over into a clump of small trees. You rush swiftly to her aid. Head-over-teacups, skis askew, she's laughing so hard she's crying. She rolled over and over so far under some pine-smelling evergreens that she's hidden from view of the rest of the skiers. After you've disengaged her from the awkward position and straightened her sun goggles, she insists on fellatio! How do you say "No" or resist an Aries woman? An Aries woman in love with love and . . . you!

TAURUS (April 20— May 20)

The Taurus Man

Recognition

The general physiognomy of the Taurus man is square. The forehead is wide, as is the mouth, with both the upper and lower lips very full and sensuous. The nose can be any length, upturned perhaps, but seldom slender; it is always full through the nostril area, suggesting a bull (what else?).

The look of the face is open, suggesting an honesty, a sureness, an attitude above reproach. Taureans very rarely carry a cross look or an expression signifying temper. The lips are usually upturned—if not smiling, then at least in a pleasant attitude. When he speaks, it's with a determined finality, as if his words are said in a bond; Taureans seldom lie.

The Taurean man must be careful not to overindulge in one of his favorite pastimes—eating. If he does, his prominent jaw can become jowled, and double chins are inevitable. If he's careful, however, and watches his weight, if he exercises regularly, takes the vitamins and minerals he should (but is apt to ignore in middle age or later), then you can usually spot him by that prominent, heavyset jaw. His eyes will usually be beautiful, almost perfect circles. The Taurus man is a great listener and capable of immense understanding. He may calculate ahead on what you're saying, and his eyes show it. Taureans are usually terrible poker players; they're entirely incapable of harboring deception.

The sign of the bull carries through in his usually wavy hair. He's likely to have the same problem as the bull itself, a forelock between the eyes.

Although his other features are large and prominent, his ears will be small and flat against the side of his head. The complexion tends to be olive or tan. Some may have lighter skin and hair, but most bulls tend toward the dark, with the eyes probably hazel or dark brown.

The term "bull-like" neck is very apropos. The Taurean usually has a very short, wide, muscular neck, which sits firmly on broad, square shoulders. Whether he's thin or plump, there's a square look about him, very solid, especially through the chest. His arms are muscular, his hands are firm. His fingers are shorter than most, but not necessarily stubby. His well-developed hands have a protective look; they're just as capable of handling a plow as caressing a woman.

Whatever his height (he runs in all sizes), he's extremely well-porportioned. He's a strong-looking, feet-on-the-ground type. Although he invariably walks with a decided stride, it's usually at a slow pace, taking in everything around him, carefully eyeing the obstacles in his path. His mind is usually on the moment, not indulging a dream or reflecting on what's past. He'll notice the beauty of architecture around him, whether a building is finished or not. He's likely to be interested in how something is going to look when it's finished, and enjoys the picturesque scene of men working, handling machinery, and creating.

He's usually a fine dancer, capable of intricate steps, and feels just as secure on a rolling ship or scaling the side of a mountain as he does on a firm dance floor. The Taurus male is cautious only in that he makes certain what is before him before he moves ahead.

Green is one of his favorite colors, but then, anything to do with earth shades appeals to the Taurean. He wears a lot of blue and brown, and reacts emotionally to pinks, mauves, light purples, and other rosy hues. Of all the zodiac signs, the Taurean is the one who most enjoys the possession of beautiful things. He is adept at determining what is phony and what is real. An *objet d'art* in an antique store can propel him into raptures of delight. It might be something of delicate crystal or a beautiful necklace handed down through generations of French or Italian families. He usually requires this sort of beauty; it's an important part of his life to have items of value and loveliness around him.

He's ironic, this bull of a guy. He seems so basically masculine, so down-to-earth, practical, and very sure. But he loves pampering baths in tepid water. He'll even sprinkle in some of his girlfriend's bath salts. He likes to keep his body soft and well-oiled, and is extremely fond of male-scent perfumes. It's very rare to find a Taurean who doesn't appreciate beautiful aromas, particularly in the bath. His choice of soap, shaving lotion, and hair tonic will most definitely be of the same fragrance.

The Taurean indulges in romantic visions, but they're very deep down inside him. He'll never display this feeling until he knows you extremely well.

Where his clothing is concerned, you can rest assured he probably won't have a multitudinous wardrobe. What is there, however, will be of the finest materials. He likes soft things, fine cashmere jackets and shirts made of the best silks. The cotton in the underclothing or shorts he wears will most likely be pima cotton; sports clothes will be soft fabrics that never feel rough against his skin.

More often than not his clothes will be dominated by shades of blue and brown, or a combination of the two. With many Taurean men there's almost a compulsion for these colors.

Where to Find Him

The choice of careers for this man can be truly at opposite ends of the aesthetic pole. The more artistic side of him will find joy and fulfillment in a musical career. He may be a fine artist or sculptor. You'll find a lot of Taurus men at the neighborhood playhouse, doing any job available. His tastes run to symphonic and classical music.

At the other end of the scale, he's equally successful in the field of banking, especially handling loan situations. He has an astute mind when it comes to finances, and if you've got problems in that field, you'll usually find a Taurean ready to help you solve them. He has the patience to listen and the good judgment needed to give you advice.

If you're looking for an apartment or house, check around for a real-estate office harboring a Taurean. Because of their faculty for honesty, many of them are in the law field, and they are successful there because of their ability to follow through, however slowly and steadily they progress. If you'd like to meet and know a Taurean, brush up on your typing and shorthand and get an executive secretary's job in a law office. He'll most likely be there, either as a junior partner or as the top man himself.

You'll find the Taurean at symphony concerts, in museums, or in antique shops. He may be found staring at something like a bejeweled comb dating back to 4 B.C. and practically entranced at the discovery. Ask him questions. You don't have to be too informed; get him talking on his favorite subject, and you're in!

Pragmatic he is, and when he's had it, he's had it! When he's up to his eyeballs in tension, no matter whether he's a musician or a financier, he knows his breaking point and packs up for a fishing trip. If you see a sign "Gone Fishin'" on a door, the author is more than likely a Taurean. He loves getting away from the world, seeking out quiet places with mossy glens and trickling brooks well-stocked with trout. He likes solitude and will be particular about the spot he chooses. If you should bump into him in or around some glassy blue lake, let *him* catch the fish. *You* rave about it. He loves camping out, be it in a camper or a tent. He'll park in the woods and just revel in nature and the earthiness around him. If you're a gypsy sort, park your van or trailer in any state park or remote area, and more often than not you'll find the Taurus male, hiking, seeking out and thoroughly enjoying the intriguing aspects of nature.

You'll find him at a football game appreciating the man-against-man struggle, the intellectual aspects of the game, knowing the proper move at the proper time, and really reconnoitering the scene to ascertain what's the best move against a defenseless team.

Primary Move

After you've recognized and discovered this guy, go after him through love of art and his stomach. Tell him, "I've got some interesting etchings by a Spanish artist that I'd like you to see, and I'd like you to advise me about their value."

This sort of invitation is bound to intrigue him. Once you've got him home, offer him escargot or lobster. Just tell him a friend in Maine sent them to you!

This guy loves good home cooking, and he can enjoy it at a table sitting by the fire, or even eating from a TV table.

He's no fussy gourmet, so his hostess can start him off with an Italian salad, a real antipasto with herbs, anchovies, provolone, and radishes. He likes the homey, down-to-earth foods, so after the salad topped with vinegar and oil, oregano and salt, he'll be ready for steak, lamb chops, or roast beef with potatoes. He likes potatoes prepared in any manner. He loves eating desserts smothered in wild toppings, like vanilla ice cream topped with a fruit potpourri or with bananas, coconut, and whipped cream.

If food is served artistically, his interest is piqued and can swing him into second helpings even if he's on a diet. He's got a ravenous appetite. He likes his soup served thick in a real tureen, with the proper spoons. His steak should be served on a hot metal platter, sizzling in its own juices. His salad belongs only in a wooden bowl. Even if everything isn't as tasty as it should be, his artistic sense is alert while dining, so take a cue: present it attractively.

In the drinking department, he is a connoisseur of wines, enjoying not only the fine taste, but the aroma as well. He likes to consult with the wine steward in a fine restaurant, discussing the year and conditions of growth. While his interest in food is more gourmand than gourmet, he really appreciates good, expensive wines, and insists on the proper glass.

He has a penchant for the finest in blended whiskey, for excellent Scotch, for aged bourbon. You can't fool him on these potables. He knows the taste and the smell, and can also gauge the socko feeling he derives from each.

After dinner, if you have tickets to the opera or symphony, ask him to join you. He may very well know you're making a pass, but he'll realize you're trying to please him as well, and he'll accept readily.

A word of caution: Don't flirt while you're with a Taurus man! A Taurean cannot abide women who "make eyes" or "carry on" with other men. If you're with him and guilty of this, you'll lose him immediately. Direct all your attention towards him, because if he's put off, he may not show it by anger or words, but he'll tighten up in a cold manner. And you'll never hear from him again.

Focus all your attention on him. Take him home and sit down by the fireside again. Suit his fancy through a combination of femininity and direct approach. Let your desires take a second place. Your aim to please should take precedence over everything else.

Pre-coitus

One of the interesting facets of a Taurean's disposition that is not obvious to many people is his involvement in music and art. He may not know what he's looking at (although some Taurean men are well-educated in the area), but he has a tremendous sensitivity, sort of an antenna that taps into the good and truly artistic. Color, too, is extremely meaningful in his life.

On this night when you plan to bed the bull, it really doesn't matter what the surroundings are, as long as they're comfortable. Even if you don't have a dime and you live in a one-room apartment, he doesn't care as long as the music is playing and the lights are soft. You could, however, light a little incense burner. The exotic aromas filling the room make his senses react immediately. The Taurean's mind works like a calculator; first impressions can be very important. A fireplace will really turn him on.

It's thought that the Taurean male is impassive, that he isn't overt or overly interested where women are concerned. This is a fallacy. The Taurean male is very much attracted to the opposite sex, but women must approach him—not aggressively, but with femininity. Ask him what he thinks about those paintings, how he likes his music, who are his favorite disc jockeys, what kind of food he enjoys. If a woman talks along these lines, in no time at all the Taurean male will open up. His basic nature is an artistic one manifested by extreme generosity and kindness. His stubbornness is awakened only as a control to anger. If he becomes obstinate, even for no apparent reason, stop cold or he'll lose his temper and you can write off the relationship.

There's one other thing you must watch when dealing with the sign of the bull. Avoid teasing him ... about anything. He can get sexually turned off under such conditions. You'll find he'll just sit there, arms folded; he'll be waiting for just a moment or two to pull his ends together and make a fast exit.

To please his sense of the beautiful and artistic, wear a long, tight-fitting dress which shows off your figure, yet is loose-flowing around the legs. Your color choice can run from an ethereal mauve to a pale blue or an enchanting shade of jade green. The top of the gown should be of a sheer, flimsy material, ruffled and open to the waist, with a demure pin holding the neckline in place. Then only with certain movements can he catch a glimpse of the roundness of your breasts or the outline of the nipples. Long sleeves with ruffled cuffs circling soft hands with carefully manicured nails really add to his pleasure. Make sure there is no chipped nail polish or sloppiness about grooming that night.

Your dress should be slit to the knee or to the hip so that your thigh is exposed as you cross your legs. Be sure to keep your shoes on; he likes to see the total woman, which in his mind represents the epitome of womanhood. He loves long hair, casually done, so if yours is short, try wearing a fall. He won't mind if you have to take it off before you get into bed. As long as there is no phony bosom padding. He doesn't care if your false eyelashes slip, or your lipstick smears, once you're bedded. Ladies not endowed with full breasts have nothing to be concerned about with the bull. He likes it as he sees it, so don't pull any surprises in that area.

When he walks over to your chair and sits on the arm and holds your hand in his, don't pull yours away. This is the beginning with the Taurean male. He'll squeeze your hand gently. Then he'll put his arm around your shoulder, while his other hand will hold your upper arm. There's just a hint of sexuality at this point. As he's holding your upper arm, he'll obviously let the back of his hand press against your breast, letting his fingers arouse your nipple. He can continue to fondle your nipple and continue to talk just as if it were as natural as could be. Go along with the unusual love approach; he's very affectionate.

Then, very naturally, he'll encompass you in a bear hug, pulling you bodily out of the chair. You'll feel every part of his body next to yours. You may also discover that as your blood pressure went up, his penis has made a firm outline against his trousers. You'll feel it practically digging into you. Most Taureans are very muscular, and the penis is no exception.

He'll kiss you then, but no butterfly kisses! Forget you are a lady and extend your tongue into his mouth. Let his tongue meet yours vigorously as he crushes his mouth against yours. Bite his lower lip, but don't draw blood. Let him know you're ready as you hotly press your body against his.

Coitus

Now the Taurean will really commence to kiss you like you've never been kissed before. Once he has truly started, he cannot hold back. After he's calculated that this is someone he wants, he's not shy; he'll go immediately into sensuous French kissing. He'll practically devour your face with his mouth. By now you'll be half-undressed, with pieces of clothing trailing you into the bedroom. He's a no-nonsense guy who, with one hand, can manipulate that pin on your dress, while his other hand is busy stroking your vulva. His fingers will explore your vagina as his thumb strokes your clitoris —all this from the armchair to the bed! The Taurean makes the kind of love that's recorded for posterity in books, but he expects your participation and reciprocation. He doesn't mind doing almost all the work, if he sees a reaction. Show him; react and love it. Enjoy it all, because he'll let you know exactly what he wants. He'll either tell you quietly, whispering in your ear, or ask you outright while you're lying in bed to put your legs around his hips while he kneels between them. Almost magically he'll have your legs moved from his hips up on his shoulders, with two foam pillows placed perfectly under your rear end. He'll brace himself by placing his legs farther apart as he thrusts his penis determinedly into your vagina, his arms placed on either side of your body supporting his frame as he moves his hips in a fast, frantic motion. When he's climaxed, he'll be careful not to put his full weight on your body. One part of his mind will always function in a practical manner.

Restimulate him now, his way. He's a very methodical lover, so in your persuasive way, be very complete and methodical in your lovemaking. Hold his penis in your hand, first massaging the head, then the length of the shaft. Voluptuously touch the testicles and knead them gently in an almost businesslike methodical manner.

It's interesting, too, that you can do to a Taurus male what most men would enjoy doing to you. Do nibble at his breasts; he finds this most wonderful. Fellatio is always in order with the Taurean, but again, do it methodically.

It's a funny thing, but he can stop in the middle of a sexual involvement and say, "Let's have a cigarette or something to drink." He likes to prolong these lovely affairs. So if he stops you like this, he's not uninterested, he is just taking his time. As a gourmet sits before a magnificent dinner, so a Taurean male sits before a beautiful sexual situation.

After he's had his cigarette, blowing smoke rings and putting the third finger of your left hand through them, he will be the aggressive one, as before. Interrupting sex at this point relaxes him, and in this way he can prepare himself physically for the denouement, the very masterpiece of sexual expression. Don't let the interruption turn you off, because after it, he'll be ready again. The Taurean can delay orgasm for as long as he desires. In most cases, he, of all signs, is most adept at this. It's advisable then to realize that you must get a lot of sleep the night before your first experience. It takes a lot of strength to deal with a Taurean male when he's ready, because when he is, he'll take over one hundred percent. Sometimes the takeover comes by his approaching you vehemently. He'll make demands such as, "Get up on your knees and come to the edge of the bed. Straighten up!" As he's commanding, he'll stand on the floor in front of you, then kneel with one leg on the bed and at the same time sink his penis to the very hilt in your vagina, spreading your legs in some way you never knew they could go as he enters you for the final thrust. A burst of rockets accompanies his final orgasm, with his voice and maleness as a trumpet tattooing his ecstasy in you.

Post-coitus

When it's over, just snuggle in his arms. You don't have to do much talking. He'll do the talking. He'll talk philosophy, he'll talk about the dinner he enjoyed. He may even discuss the wondrous experience you just had together, without trying to arouse you sexually. He has a great propensity for describing how he felt when you nibbled at his nipples and what it was like when he had his final ejaculation. He'll make you feel as though you were the ultimate sex partner for him and that your prowess at sex was naturally stimulated by his manhood.

Just agree with him, kiss him sweetly all over his face, stretch like a satisfied pussycat, and say goodnight as you fall off to sleep. He won't be offended; he'll be happy thinking he exhausted you.

The Taurus Women

Recognition

In this mad world of temporary decisions, fast change, and deliberate indifference, the Taurean woman is a refreshing relief.

She looks tall, no matter what her height, which is usually short to medium, and carries herself with assuredness, not aggressively at all, but with a true certainty. Likewise, she's basically honest and sincere as a person, filled to the brim with integrity and kindness.

Her face is square, and so is the jaw, the eyebrows in contrast greatly arched, framing round, beautiful eyes, never too large, but exceedingly calm. Many Taurean women have a heavy-lidded, "bedroomy" look. This look, combined with their sureness, is pertinent to the Taurean being—totally sensual as opposed to sexual. There's nothing subtle or ephemeral about their tastes or feelings.

The neck is short and full, the nose small and pert. Her ears are tiny and lovely, set close to the head, and she's extremely proud of them, adorning them with exquisite earrings. Her mouth is large and well-shaped, expressive, with beautifully formed lips. Her hair is her outstanding feature, though, lustrous and usually dark. More often than not her forehead is distinguished with a decided widow's peak, of which she's inordinately proud and rarely camouflages it with bangs or curls. And she's fortunate in that her hair won't turn gray until late in life.

Her torso is large, with a broad back, full hips, well-developed breasts tending to suggest a solid look as opposed to fat and sloppy. But because she carries herself so well, the

Taurean woman's weight is tough to ascertain. She may look 115 and really weigh 125.

She resents being rushed, and this quality is apparent in the way she walks, never dawdling, but just relaxed, enjoying life as she saunters through it. She lives a cyclical life, her persistence and enormous energy demanding that she finish everything she starts, even if it's just an ordinary stroll around the block.

This lady makes a great and patient friend who'll sit for hours and listen to your problems and stories. If you're just looking for sympathy, however, she'll let you have it. But if she's genuinely interested and feels there's a way to help, she'll wheedle out of you exactly what the trouble is. She's excellent with nervous and highly tense people, able to relax them with ease. Once you're her friend, however, she becomes extremely possessive and will take over in the area of advice, assuring you she knows the key to your happiness. And you know, ninety-nine percent of the time she's right!

The Taurean woman is not one to be hung up about small matters. She's calm, placid, and possessed of a logical thinking machine, forming a pattern for herself of accomplishing her aims. She's highly tenacious and dislikes change.

If you cross her, however, there's a terrible temper lying in wait. If you lie or don't fulfill a promise, or try to defeat some of her humanitarian aims, her rage is equal to that of her sign, the mad bull! But her temper is lost only with good reason. She utilizes no so-called feminine wiles, no fluttering eyelashes, no tears, no tricks. There's no shoddiness about her. She's one hundred percent woman, with a mind of her own.

Most Taurean females are just the opposite of the spoiled brat. They're well-adjusted and handle their own lives and those of others quite well. She does love to possess expensive things, though. Some of the time she'll use self-restraint, but if wealthy, her closets will be filled with high-style clothes. She resembles the Leo woman in this respect, and like Ms. Leo, wants good furnishings around her, but also those that are long-lasting. She likes the feel of nubby fabrics, shantung or English tweed. She adores the furry feeling of cashmere, or the glistening, watered pattern of *peau de soie*. Colors? Well, she's adamant about the rosy-pink family of shades, and will highlight this cheery color with a scarf in citron yellow or electric blue.

The price tag's important on perfumes, too, and she prefers fresh, natural scents and odors alive with floral accents. She likes clean and sparkling fragrances like the smell of the world after a spring rain. If she's not born wealthy, she'll earn enough to buy what she wants, and goes directly to the source.

Substance and quantity are important when it comes to food for the Taurean lady. No fancy foreign tidbits for her, no exotic tastes to mar the basics. She's a steak-and-potato gal, not much for subtle sauces. Craves the best of breads, though—rye, pumpernickel, Syrian, and homemade. In the vegetable line, she goes for definitive flavors like cauliflower, brussels sprouts, or cabbage. Give her a salad with chunks of tomato and cucumbers, perhaps some onion, and a simple dressing.

When it comes to desserts, lay it on heavy with fancy, creamy items like pies, ice cream, and cake, but forget about flambés.

Where to Find Her

Look in art galleries, especially those devoted to contemporary works, to find the Taurean woman. She enjoys both the drama of color used explosively and the sensuous look and appeal of sculpture to the point of touching it as though it were alive.

Her practical side could guide her in the paths of banking, clerking, and holding down an executive position. Where there's money, there she'll be! She has a second sense equipped to smell it out. She's excellent at drawing up contracts, and makes a fine lawyer.

You'll likely find her on long hikes through woods, or bicycling down some rural path. She's an avid bird-watcher, and has a ball at a carnival or circus. Look for her to be the most joyous female on the Ferris wheel, roller coaster, or merry-go-round.

Her sense of organization is incredible in the administrative field. She's a bit slow, but determined, never leaving anything undone. Because farms require intense organization for productive operation, The Taurean female can very well be found "down on the farm," a gentlewoman farmer with a mind for detail.

No matter where you look, you'll find the Taurean woman involved in some sort of artistic endeavor. She may toil tirelessly through the day, but at night she'll require a creative outlet like painting, preferably watercolor landscapes. She may be a book collector, and loves classical music.

Primary Move

Emotional fondness in the Taurean woman, when it turns to love, becomes a long-lasting commodity for her. Once you decide you want to score, be prepared to finish the game. While others weary of the battle to succeed, this lady never tires. Total dependability is her virtue, and she'll generally never stray.

But if she is angered, forget the whole thing. Her affection will quickly cool, and she won't give you a second chance. As a love object you will become as stale as yesterday's news. In short, you'll be out, with no possible opportunity to rekindle that old flame or restore that old feeling. That's just her nature, pure and simple.

If the Taurean girl doesn't apply self-control in her early life, her sexual and sensual desires can run away with her. But if she's learned self-restraint, she's no one to toy with. If you come on strong with her, be sure you follow through!

Wonderfully down-to-earth, yet aesthetically aware, the Taurean woman is open to ideas and thoughts of nature. Don't lead her down the garden path; make it a woodsy trail on foot or via bicycle, and you'll get the benefit or her love of nature and its wonders. Suggest a picnic on a farm, offer solid foods, and her defenses will be lowered. She'll be dressed simply but expensively even for this rural jaunt, so honor the occasion with your best sports outfit.

After your al fresco lunch, suggest a walk, and don't be a bit hesitant about holding her hand or putting your arm around her shoulders. When you're facing the inevitable sunset, where nature displays a riot of color and beauty, kiss her, for her sensual warmth is at its peak. However, you haven't won her yet. The Taurean woman loves an extravagant man, and she's likely to make some outrageous demand before giving herself to you. Whatever she demands, try to satisfy her. You'll find that whatever your investment, the Taurean lady will see to it that your returns in pleasure will be greater by far.

Pre-coitus

To check out your sincerity (not to mention your financial situation), the Taurean might suggest that you take a trip together. What could be more exciting than beginning a new affair in a foreign country? And what country could be more romantic than sun-drenched Italy? All right, the reservations are made, your passports are in order, and the day comes when you and your exotic Taurean lady step off the plane into the Italian sunshine.

You immediately step into a private limousine, avoiding the rest of the sightseers, and instruct the driver in your best Italian to take you to a mountaintop to see the view. As the car careens crazily over those serpentine Italian roads, dizzily turning on a dime to prevent a fall into the chasms below, she's thrown on your lap, and you're thrown on hers. That's a switch, and she loves the bodily contact.

As the driver goes his mad pace, neither of you is getting the benefit of the exquisite view or the flavor of the people who inhabit the little villas along the way.

You're wrapped in each other. First, just the smiles, then the hands, then the arms flung about each other in ardent embrace. You wonder and ask the driver how long time-wise it will take to the peak. "Eh?" he says. "How much time, how long to the top of the mountain?" you shout above the squeaking and caterwauling of the tires as they swerve around the bends in the road. "Oh! *Quindici minuti,*" he laughs back, enjoying your hand tricks to make known to him what you want. "Mmmm, fifteen minutes, there's time, then," you think, "and the driver's too occupied with keeping his vehicle under control to notice or care what's happening with his passengers."

She knows what's going on in your mind and doesn't object. The very thought of coitus on the floor of the back of the car turns her on, particularly with the chauffeur bumbling along, cursing under his breath as two goats briskly trot across the road, causing a short stop and a slamming of brakes.

This interlude gives you an opportunity to take the car rugs folded in the back of the limousine and lay them on the floor. Ah, there's a snug crib. While the driver is busy grinding gears and negotiating the sudden curves, you are even busier negotiating the equally wild curves of your Taurus lady.

What a wild ride. No self-exertion as the movement of the car pushes and pulls your bodies in a rocking motion. Sometimes it does require a bit of hand manipulation to keep your penis properly inserted, particularly when the driver goes directly over a couple of large rocks.

Your Taurus lady is oblivious to all except the constant pounding of your body against and in her.

Suddenly the driver is shouting, "*Adesso noi habbiamo venuto!*" (Now we come.) Yes, as he brakes the car too quickly, you do! And it's one for history as she sends out those almost invisible silken threads, like a spider, capturing you in her Taurean web. And you love it.

Knees shaking, bodies shivering with the past passion of lovemaking in such an unusual circumstance, you're both ready to spend the day engrossed in seeing the sights, as carefree and gay as two people who have some special bond between them, sharing a special secret.

Coitus

The day leads into glorious night, and dinner is available at the little inn just around the bend. Two whole days in this enchanted village, two whole days on this magic mountain.

Dinner is served in a simple dining room boasting intimate booths. You are dining in a fashion reminiscent of the Tom Jones fable. The Taurus lady nibbles on the chicken leg, biting into its succulent meat and chewing with enjoyment; her eyes are sparkling. Then her tongue slithers across her upper lip in full pleasure. The chicken leg's not that good. She's enjoying fantasy fellatio, and making no bones about it. Taking her cue, you raise an oyster on its open shell to your lips and lasciviously loosen it from the shell with your tongue. You slowly suck it into your mouth and then swallow it with relish. She's laughing now and feeling your tongue within her. Cunnilingus is her favorite spectator sport. Not to be outdone by your performance, she busies herself with slowly and purposefully sucking on the claw of a crab, ostensible to extract the tender meat. But you both know that in her mind it's the head of your penis that is getting all this attention.

After sexually feasting on the specialties of the house and imbibing local wine, you're both ready to retire, anxious to play your fantasy feast for real. Too sensuously stimulated and

The Lovers' Guide to Sensuous Astrology 33

happily groggy to traipse down the mountain and renew your back-seat screwing, you decide to spend the night at this little inn. The driver's most agreeable to stay the night, the extra lire help. As you walk the staircase together, surrendering the dining room to those less fortunate than yourselves, you await with great anticipation the remainder of this night. A Taurus woman suffers frequent disappointment. Her realization is sometimes so much less than she expects. Tonight that is not the case. Her fondest hopes and desires are to be realized.

The room is rustic, furnished with an old-fashioned four-poster bed, mattressed in eiderdown. The washstand with pitcher and bowl is the extent of plumbing in the room. Down the hall is the toilet facility, serving five rooms of the ten at the inn. But your eyes cursorily take in the wardrobe, the stool, the small chair, and the candlesticks. You're more interested in each other as you walk together toward the jumbo quilts.

There's a clutching at each other to know the entire body of each, having already known the pleasure of crazy-car coitus and the extent of each other's erotic imagination.

She removes her blouse and skirt. The bra strap catches on the bedpost and merrily whirls down to the bed. Holding up her off-black hose is a singularly stunning garterbelt laced with intertwining black ribbon.

Most women buy pantyhose; not our Taurean. She loves the look of her hips encased in black lace, long elastic garters to the tops of her hose. With panties off, she's right, and you can't resist rubbing your face in the lovely picture framed by lingerie.

Her vivid drive stimulates you to more inventive foolery. You open the wardrobe door and stand her on the bottom, legs spread in a reverse Y, feet touching each side of the closet, arms raised to the top in a Y. Pulling a little stool close to her pouting vulva, you resume your feast, but in reality this time, enjoying each tidbit as you find it moistened with her local brew.

Unable to stand this fantastic nerve-wracking devouring any further without participating herself, she steps down from the wardrobe, and while you're still sitting on the stool, she impales herself on your penis. Homing in carefully, she proceeds to whirl her hips around as breezily as the bra strap on the bedpost. She grinds her hips down and around, up and off, in and out, enjoying her ride as much as her mountain-road motor trip. The scene in the dining room was just a snack compared to the banquet you are enjoying now.

Post-coitus

Practically crawling to the four-poster, you both collapse into the downy softness. She embraces you closer, closer to her, and falls sound asleep. Nothing to talk about. It's all been said, but you think as she lies there close and lovely near you: "What a fantastic woman. Novelty and devotion, love and adventure, what more could a man ask?"

"But what's that tight and heavy feeling around my ankle?"

"Nothing, just my imagination, I guess."

Not so, it's the iron anklet and the first few links of the ball and chain you asked for ... and got.

GEMINI (May 21–June 21)

The Gemini Man

Recognition

In culling out the Gemini man from all the other signs of the zodiac, look for a face that's usually slender, streamlined, angled somewhat, and elongated. The forehead is almost always quite high, relating to his lightning-fast brain. Most Gemini are very intellectual.

The Gemini man has an "in-motion" look about him, as if he's about to take off momentarily, reflecting the Mercurial part of his sign.

His nose is usually long and thin. The mouth is usually wide, but not full. The lips range from average to very thin, and like the rest of the Gemini man, are frequently in motion. When you converse, he will be doing most of the talking—in quick, short sentences—as if his mind is way ahead of his speech.

The earlobes of the Gemini man are quite long, but rarely prominent; the ears are usually proportionally placed and do not extend far from the side of the head.

The hair of the Gemini man is of particular interest, most likely within the brunette shades, and usually not worn in overly exaggerated lengths. Don't count too heavily on the color of hair when looking for your Gemini man. They come in all shades.

His body is most likely slender and tall, with more of the athletic bearing of a runner, pacer, or oarsman as opposed to a wrestler. This lengthy leanness adds to his appearance of movement or swiftness. Gemini are not exactly graceful by definition, but they dart quickly; you may suddenly turn around and find them gone. You can usually pick them out easily by watching for their rapid staccato movements. To catch one, you may have to try to match his quick strides.

Although his shoulders can be broad, they tend to slope and are carried slightly forward, giving a fluid appearance. The legs are usually slender, and muscled in the way of a swimmer rather than a weightlifter. Most Gemini men have a lean and elegant look.

His fingers are often long, and again, constantly in motion, as if clutching at invisible objects. Visible things too: playing with a pencil while talking, winding a clock, and fiddling with papers are Gemini giveaways. A lot of Gemini men use worry beads in their offices as well as at home, as if they're constantly working off excess energy. If they cross and uncross their legs a great deal, they're not neurotic; they're simply devoted to constant animation of their extremities.

The Gemini man can put together a wardrobe that is absolutely striking, avant-garde perhaps, but never way, way out. He will usually go for any new "in" look, any "mod" fashion, and can achieve a dapper appearance no matter what he wears.

His tastes in clothing are expensive, and even if he's not wealthy, he'll put aside a goodly amount for clothing. Green is usually his favorite color among the altogether optimistic hues he likes. When it comes to color coordination, he's great. When dressing for business, he will be the epitome of perfection, choosing a conservative tone but stressing cut and style above all. He's a good relative to have: he grows tired of clothes quickly and is generous about giving them away.

He's usually too anxious and in a hurry when it comes to jewelry. Wearing perhaps a school ring will suffice. Sometimes he omits a wristwatch, preferring, if he is wearing a vest, to wear a pocket watch.

In cologne, lotion, or perfume, his tastes go to very sharp scents, bright and clean as opposed to anything exotic or mysterious. Deodorant, shaving cream, hair dressing, and soap will have the same aroma, reminiscent of forests and the freshness of the out-of-doors.

Every hair is usually in place, because he spends ample time to achieve a well-groomed look. His nails are either manicured or scrupulously self-cared-for. The full effect of the Gemini man is one approaching perfection in grooming, style, and color coordination.

Where to Find Him

You are most likely to find this energetic and curious "twin" combination man at hunting lodges, ski lodges, or at just about any sporting event. He loves to water-ski, handle boats, or fly planes. You'll be sure to find him at the opening games of the football or baseball season, but his impatience may remove him from that arena after the first few thrills. Although his enthusiasm may wane in mid-season, he'll definitely be back in the stadium for the final performance. A Gemini is fascinated with seeing who draws first blood and who winds up the victor, but the in-between seesaw battle leaves him cold.

He usually prefers being a participant. Tennis is a good game for him; golf is often too slow. Wherever there's swift physical involvement for the individual, you'll find the Gemini man. His insatiable curiosity and wide-ranging interests put him under the sea in scuba gear just as readily as flying a plane five miles up in the sky. Despite his questioning nature, he may easily lose interest in a subject or a sport once he's explored every avenue of it. A man who requires constant progress, he wants to get on to the next challenge.

Career-wise, Gemini men are drawn to varied fields encompassing public relations, advertising, sales, or entrepreneurial activities. There's practically no organization that doesn't house the Gemini, but you can be sure he'll be doing many different things, all at the same time, equally well.

The Gemini man is well-suited to law enforcement. The constant action and challenge captures his imagination and puts his multifaceted skills to good use. It's more than probable he may be in the scientific areas of logic or personnel administration.

Culturally, his admiration for music and drawing could entice him to study in special classes. He could start class with determination, but, alas, he could lose interest fast when lessons must be constantly repeated.

He loves to dance; he'll be attracted to the nice places where the band plays until dawn. He rarely visits singles bars or pickup spots, preferring to bring a date who's a good dancer and as tireless as he is.

The fields of public relations and advertising are probably

abounding with Gemini men. Their ability to write succinctly and humorously suits them for these fields.

They can debate a point and lecture convincingly. Politics is a good possibility with Gemini, but in this case the long-term grind, saying or doing the same things over and over again, is out. It's contact with many people in all walks of life that stirs him.

Primary Move

After you've searched for, recognized, and are ready to approach your flighty prospective catch, some important facts to keep in mind are his patterns of dining and drinking.

In the food department, he's somewhat picky, but only because he craves the rare and exotic. He will try anything at least once, mainly for the sheer fun and experience. He's a nibbler, loves hors d'oeuvres, even prefers them to heavy, multicourse meals. He loves to try new and odd things like snails, snake meat, buffalo, bear, and so forth. He'll eat spinach, but it's got to be fixed creatively. He enjoys spices, herbs, onions, poppy seed, vinegar, chives, pimiento, or buttermilk when utilized in preparing a dish. Gourmet restaurant-going is a favorite occupation, and he just might ignore an entrée after checking on all the exotic appetizers, choosing two or three, and dining on them with relish.

The Gemini man's taste in liquor generally leans to straight whiskey, and he usually does not consume a great deal at a time. Perhaps two short drinks, and then he'll wait. His drink tastes are actually very simple, and he drinks merely to enjoy. He needs no artificial stimulation from liquor. He has enough innate ebullience. Gemini's simply inspired by living and by anything that's new and progressive.

The Gemini man will appreciate and expect directness. He will find you far more desirable if you're turned onto things that interest him. Even if you have to read the *Farmer's Almanac*, archaeology, or Proust to innovate conversation—be prepared!

He's not particularly concerned with the mechanics of tennis or baseball. It's the excitement of the results that fascinates him. He likes to know and discuss champions. He will expect you to know that six-love is a tennis score, not a sexual achievement or variation. Show enthusiasm for what he likes, but make sure it's genuine. Some reconnoitering about him as to his preferences will pay off in the long run.

If he invites you to a baseball game, turn around and invite him to another sport, like jai alai, soccer, or boat racing—anything that will involve him as a participant or an aroused observer. If it's chess or even an intellectually oriented political talk, be as fully informed as he. His creative makeup embraces an extraordinary interest in planning and construction of a community. If he decides it would be just great to attend a city commission meeting concerning development of parks and playgrounds for children, do more than just tag along. Do some library homework to find out just how badly they're needed in your city. His amazement will be topped only by his admiration for you.

If one of your hobbies is catching and mounting butterflies, extend an invitation to him to see how you do it. Some pertinent photos of you tramping through the field with your net and some documented awards for treasures you've mounted will pique his interest. Either way, whether it's by your invitation or his motivation, after contact has been made, he'll take over. It's up to you, though, to continue to be knowledgeable and keep the interest on a high level.

Pre-coitus

Since we know Gemini men are mentally agile, very excitable, and have wonderful conversational ability, they're easy to recognize. They enjoy experimentation and make good investigators. They like to be busy and are usually youthful and up-to-date in their outlook and appearance.

New, exotic outfits that are dramatic and novel will amuse him. He has a great wit, so there can be a gay and carefree attitude toward sex with a Gemini man.

Dress up as Mata Hari—covered up to the neck, but with your breasts exposed, nipples tinted pink. Wear a plain flannel nightie, with the back cut out so that the cheeks of your rear end are revealed. This get-up will so delight him he'll no doubt nip your hind cheeks with his teeth or pinch them. After entertaining in naughty-nightie, become an Indian maiden with a feather tucked in a band around your forehead, an Indian beaded belt around your bare waist, with soft moccasins on your feet. Nothing else. Continue the freaky fashion show. Put on high-heel boots, a leather dress and a hat, and come out with a riding whip in your hand. The whip will stimulate visions of flagellation. Steer him into doing this gently and it can be fun. He'll love it. The unusual, the bizarre, are tantalizing to a Gemini man. He can be tempted to be all things to all women. Don Juan is the oft-quoted example of the Geminian lover who can be fickle, inconsistent, and two-faced, so you'd better prepare for a little duality, or even quadrupality. There's every possiblility you can keep him for yourself most of the time by being versatile in your approach. There's no doubt that if you want to keep this man interested in you sexually, you'll have to appeal to his mental vivaciousness. Remember, it was Don Juan's liveliness and wit that made women love him; so have plenty of your own to keep up with him.

In sexual foreplay with a Gemini, you can go into any kind of an experimental approach that you have dreamed or read about. Since this man likes to be "on top" of the latest fads and fashions, you can use a variety of accessories in the precoital stage. One such item is a tape recorder. Ask him to sit on the floor; you sit opposite him, yoga-style, and turn on the tape recorder. Tell him you're play-acting the role of the mistreated virgin and that he must do only what he is told. Then use reverse conversation as you point to the place you're describing. "I'm a pure little maiden, I'm so pure nobody wants me." As you speak, conversely lift your skirt or gown and show him you've nothing on underneath, and continue. "I never get any love, I'm a mistreated virgin . . . make me feel better!" Then take his hand across the tape recorder, and using his index and middle fingers, gently place them at the entrance of your vagina. Start the hand moving up and down, up and down. His mind will run wild with his new "role," and he'll take it from there. Continue the virgin conversation, and you'll have him believing it as you scream with delight when he "pierces" your maidenhead. Listen to that tape next time you're with him. The tape recorder won't be the only thing you turn on!

Cherry gone, kneel in front of him and deliberately remove his penis from his trousers. He may or may not have an erection at this point, but as you slowly and deliberately aim the penis toward your mouth, letting your lips part hungrily, you'll find the love machine hard in your hand. Of course, tease him—don't put it in your mouth right away. Then suck him gently, teasing with your tongue and lips . . . then stop. A Gemini lover will be interested in all the latest and most original gimmicks associated with the art of lovemaking. Bring out your private treasures and show him a French tickler suggested by the Kinsey Institute or show him two of the latest and strangest-sized and -shaped vibrators you've got.

Another way to flip the Gemini mind is to ask if he's ever seen a woman masturbate, and show him how you do it. Bet you never finish alone! Whether you're accustomed to this type of self-indulgence or not isn't important. The purpose of this action is to excite the easily bored Gemini man into a frenzy and keep him there.

You can be as aggressive as you want in sexual foreplay with this man before actual coitus. Tongue him from head to toe and in every orifice. Stick your tongue in his nostrils and let your fingers gently probe his anus. The combination of sensations will amaze and delight him. You can maneuver him into all sorts of positions by using "body English"—he'll tilt easily. You can be extremely aggressive with a Gemini man in your experimentation. He enjoys fellatio, but try various ways.

Try this one. Put enough ice in your mouth to fill the small basin of the lower palate under your tongue. Take his penis in your mouth and let it rest in the coolness. Hold it there just long enough to give it a brisk shock, then swallow the melted ice and continue aggressively massaging his penis with your lips and teeth, moving nimbly over the tip of his erection. Let your tongue deftly intrude into the orifice of his urethra. It'll drive him insane, and you can expect reciprocation—either simultaneously or when you're through. Whatever you desire, tell him. He's capable of performing cunnilingus on you persistently and untiringly until your clitoris and vagina are in full crimson flower and you're moaning in delight.

You can be weird about the choice of place with a Gemini man, too. It makes no difference if you're in the kitchen up against the refrigerator door or on the kitchen table. If you want to try it standing on your hands, this man will love to play cartwheel with you. It's strenuous, but if you're limber and supple enough, it sure is fun. Physically, Gemini men are light, wiry, and quick-moving; so take advantage of this and enjoy yourself to the full. Lose yourself! Forget where you are, and let yourself go!

Coitus

After you have exploited this diverse array of sexual foreplay, be cooperative with this man in coitus. Even in the kitchen leaning against the stove, whatever happens, you can still be aggressive if you just work with him. Don't worry about taking the role of the dainty, passive woman. You can continue to be as forward and active as you wish, for a Gemini man usually falls into a pattern of lovemaking where you will become so completely absorbed in each other's bodies that you'll forget where you begin and he ends! It's at this time you must become a clinging animal, doing nothing that could possibly separate your bodies. It's as if you are on a dance floor—very close to him—feeling his lead as every muscle and fiber of his body is concentrated on the rhythm of superb coitus. Don't let him out of your grasp. No moving apart of the bodies. Don't move away from him. Stay glued to this man when he moves, particularly when it's close to his time of climax. Let him feel your breasts pressed hard against him; your arms tightly wound around him; let him feel the demanding movements of your pelvis against his; wind your whole being with his. If you wish, you can get even closer to him by nibbling into his neck and nipping into his shoulder or his chest. Use the edge of your teeth firmly and meaningfully, but don't leave teeth marks. Good lovers don't leave marks!

Post-coitus

When lovemaking is over with the Gemini man, it's over. It's like the end of a startling thunderstorm—a lightning blaze and gone. The sea tranquil after its vigorous activity. That's the way it is. Don't expect romance, and don't expect too much tenderness. All he's concerned about is how you feel and if you hurt anywhere. Most likely you'll walk to the bedroom, where he'll gently arrange a pillow so your head rests easily near him, or he'll straighten the bedclothes so you won't be entangled in sheets and blankets. But he won't ask you, "How was it?" or "Was I good?" He knows it was, and he was. He'll only be concerned, more or less, that you're physically comfortable and that you feel good. He would just as soon go to sleep. After lovemaking with a Gemini man, no matter what sign you are, there's a lethargic wonder that flows through your limbs, even down to your very fingertips. A flowing off of passion so complete that the bed becomes a white cloud hanging tenuously in a midnight-blue sky. It's possible, too, that he may want to start talking about baseball or the latest subject that has caught his interest. If that's the case, pull your head together, stay relaxed, and be a good listener. But in the middle of this eloquence, if he gets up for a cigarette or a highball, and forgets to ask if you want one, just continue to enjoy him. It's no reflection on your charms that the weathervane of the Gemini's emotions points to clear skies, calm seas, and only him, alone, at the helm. That's just his way.

The Gemini Woman

Recognition

Lady Gemini is usually very tall and slender, carrying herself with decided assurance. Where all the action is, that's where the Gemini gal is going! She rarely does the obvious, no coquettish hip-wiggling or feline body slinking. She strides with a simple gracefulness and ease, a flowing of her body, as if swimming a long distance in the air.

Like a desert lizard, you'll often find her sunning herself, and she's usually quite gorgeously tan. Trying to take care of the resultant dry skin can be a problem, but nevertheless, it's worth all the time and trouble creaming and tending to her skin properly. In fact, being tall, tan, and terrific is her one submission to vanity.

Her face is most likely oval, but sometimes the chin is more pointed. Her nose can be prominent, and she may possess the profile of a Nefertiti, but it suits her face.

The famous Gemini bumps on each side of the forehead, so obvious on the Gemini man, are with her too, but with her carefully combed brown or black hair covering that part of the face, it's not so prominently seen.

The most exciting physical thing about her is her body, very much in proportion, very shapely, very youthful into middle and late age. Her eyes are far apart and shade from hazel to gray or brownish-gray. They're distinctive—alert and intelligent. Her mouth is flexible and appealing, constantly in motion, because the Gemini woman talks a veritable blue streak. Every little thought just wings through her mind like a bird taking flight through her agile mouth.

She uses her hands with an assertive grace to emphasize the points she wants to make. She's ambidextrous and could very well be brushing a speck of dust from a gentleman's jacket while she's adjusting an earring, all the while talking a mile a minute.

She's quick-witted and amusing, a marvelously alive personality who enjoys good, ripe gossip, but never the malicious sort. She'd just as soon kid you to your face, because she generally responds to the moment and how the situation hits her. The Gemini female is extremely mercurial and hard to pin down for a straight answer or decision. She may say yes right now and a day later say no. But she meant yes when she said it. She changes her mind rapidly and is restless both physically and mentally, and fantastically inquisitive, always looking for the how, what, why, where, and when of everything, from the most insignificant incident to the most massive catastrophe.

In discussing someone else's pending divorce she'll want to know why, what prompted it, and who's the antagonist. She's very like a computer, and keeping up with her think-track is tough.

Of all the finer human qualities, Gemini appreciates kindness directed at herself or others more than anything else in life. If one is thoughtful and considerate, she's their fan.

Falling in love through her emotions or because of her lover's appearance is not her way. Rather, it's what her lover does in the way of kindness, his integrity, and the concern he has for the world and its people, and what he's doing to contribute to a better life for all of mankind. She's unusual, an anachronism in this age of self-aggrandizement and me, me, me!

One minute the Gemini woman may be restless, exciting, outgoing, gregarious. She'll be very funny and witty, too, then wham—she becomes irritable, nervous, and shy. Sincere persuasion and loving understanding on the part of others will bring her around to her normal, happy self.

Clothes are rather unessential to the Gemini female. She usually doesn't care much about them except that they fit well and are clean. She affects tailored skirts, slacks, shirts, and turtlenecks and looks great in them. Frilly blouses or decorative touches like rhinestones, spangles, and beads are as unlike her as wearing an evening gown to a roller-skating rink.

Her wardrobe is as limited as it is simple, because she requires things that feed her mind rather than those which adorn her body. She loves red, white, and green. If she's quite tan, she'll wear white for a week, then not touch it again for a month. She knows her body's great on its own, with beautifully shaped breasts, slim waistline, rounded hips, long thighs and legs. She'll wear blue jeans well, with a red gingham shirt, and she's one of the few females who can wear a wrap-around bathrobe and look queenly in it.

Perfumes aren't important at all in her makeup. Because she's such a changeable person, she'll try a sweet lavender one day, then switch to something spicy or exotic the next.

It's practically the same with food, as she'll make a meal of celery and radishes one night, rummage the refrigerator the next and come up with chocolate cake and milk for dinner. It's mind over matter in this area. But she does love thick soups, like barley, cabbage, or corn chowder, anything that has a variety of tastes. She'll stock the larder with snacks rather than the makings for a full meal. She's marvelous with a can opener, and you'll find Polish ham, tuna fish, or sardines on the shelves. She'll suddenly latch on to tenderloin tips, and eat them every night for a week! Dairy products are her things, too, and she has a passion for ginger, whether it be in cookies, bread, or for flavoring a dessert.

Not much jewelry adorns this girl, but if she's wearing anything, it's likely to be earthy, big, native-made by the Indians of Mexico, Peru, or the United States. She loves the color of turquoise, jade, and particularly emerald. It's the mystery that attracts her in this sort of jewelry, especially the Egyptian look.

This wonderfully changeable, difficult-to-define lady carries her mercurial nature through the entire spectrum of her living pattern.

Where to Find Her

You're liable to be worn out looking for her, because she'll be in six different places at once. The Gemini gal will probably have either two concurrent occupations or a major one and an important avocation besides. She's intrigued by the sciences, and you'll find her in the fields of research, working in a doctor's office, eager to type long dissertations of medical subjects and be completely knowledgeable as to their meaning.

She'll pore over books on archaeology, and she'd make a marvelous schoolteacher because each newly discovered topic is a challenge to her. Instead of merely imparting words and thoughts to children, she's the sort who will excite their minds and make them reach out to learn. The Gemini woman has a great talent for languages, and will no doubt be fluent in at least two.

If you dig auto racing, you'll definitely find her around the course, because she's a daredevil. Geminis make fine authors. Their personalities, which combine a predilection for excitement, the mysterious, the amusing, and the poignant, are excellent requisites for good writers.

She's turned on by family history, by ancestry, and if she makes you a present of your family's coat-of-arms, rest assured you're A-1 on her list. She loves sports, and she's terribly involved, whether it be swimming, water-skiing, diving, or scuba exploration; and up north, sledding, ice-skating, tobogganing, or horseback riding.

Her hobbies are multitudinous, although because of her nature she'll start a lot of projects and finish few. If ceramics attracts her, she'll go all out, purchase all the necessary material, and then give it away when the project becomes tiresome. Don't waste a lot of time or money at a hobby class, because she's not likely to be there for long.

Primary Move

This romantic lady first falls in love with an idea or an ideal . . . not you! No matter how good-looking you are, no matter how fat or thin, these factors mean little. If you have the ability to stimulate her mentally, that's your proper line of attack.

Check the papers and find out when there's a lecture by a health fanatic, by a scientific explorer, or someone who's crossed the Atlantic in a rowboat. Ask her to join you, and you'll pique her interest right away. Her mind's like a sponge.

Be on time, because she'll be raring to go, terribly excited over the prospect of such an evening. Of course, she'll no doubt talk all during the lecture, and when it's over, she'll dart out of the hall because she's now ready for other things and thoughts.

Don't try a drawn-out formal dinner with this girl. The nearest good hot-dog stand will suffice. She doesn't need music, moonlight, roses, or a romantic setting. But be a Boy Scout with courtesy and kindness. Help her in and out of the theater seat, remove her coat, and be sure you sprint for her side of the car before she opens the door herself. These are the few amenities in life she really appreciates.

Snacktime over, you're way ahead. Suggest a stroll on the beach or in the park, but keep the talk going. If you've been kind, she will be, too!

Pre-coitus

Unlike her male counterpart, Gemini man, the Gemini woman is not drastically pulled in several different directions at the same time. Bored easily, of course, unless she is constantly occupied, it's not that frenetic and impatient moving about from one occupation to another. Her changeability is more logical, spontaneous only when the moment describes a switch.

Your Gemini gem is an all-around woman who will devote herself as actively to chatting about art, sculpture, and modern philosophy at a cocktail party as she will be hooking a wriggling worm on a fishing hook as she casts for trout. Her delight is in just being alive.

A camping-fishing trip is well-suited to her personality. It starts her fertile imagination flowering, and she's the kind of companion in the woods that can bend to the capricious capers of nature's whims. No hysterics if she's affronted by a wild-eyed raccoon, no squeals and jumping on camp chairs if a snake slithers by.

If you rent a good-sized camper equipped with all the comforts of home, you can have a fabulous, fun weekend awaiting you.

No need to beat around the bush. Just say it, "I've got a great wagon, I know where there's a big fish just waiting to be caught, join me?" If you set the pickup time at four A.M., there'll be no complaining from this Gemini. She's there, waiting downstairs on the street, knapsack in hand, jeans and football sweater on.

On the road your map seems to be ineffective. Routes have changed, and you find yourselves entangled in a cloverleaf traffic pattern that places you going back to the direction from which you came. Perhaps other women of the zodiac would mutter something about "The Great Pathfinder." Not Gemini. She'll revel in the unexpected turn of events and say, "It was fate!" and urge you to follow signs to the nearest fishing campsite you see. She'll be certain it'll be better than the one where you were expected.

And right she is. As you bounce down an unpaved back road, there's a weathered post with a faded sign hanging on it at a forty-five-degree angle, "Rest Haven." Now you're less that twenty feet away from a group of charming log cabins and parked campers with their canopies erected, people sprawled on camp chairs enjoying the beautiful scene of the lake and evergreeen trees dotting the shoreline. She exuberantly puts her hand on your thigh, tapping a tattoo to "There's No Business Like Show Business." You're surprised; it's an unlikely tune to be humming, but that's your Gemini. You never know what fleeting thoughts traipse through her intelligent mind to bring on these outbursts of song.

Hooked up to electricity and water in the farthest lot from the crowd, she's a helpmate unpacking the gear you brought and a sincere apprentice for the carpentry work you do to set up the brightly colored awning as a protection from the sun.

Feeling a bit weary over the hassling traffic and change of plans, your suggestion to rest awhile is offhandedly rejected. She talks you into renting a rowboat to do some midstream fishing. Untangling fishing poles and tackle, arranging your lures carefully in their places, then ready to walk to the main cabin for boat rental, mercurially she changes her mind and says, "You're right, let's rest awhile."

After settling your equipment against the side of the camp chairs, you enter the trailer. Before you have a chance to turn around and close the door to the undersized home on wheels, you find her standing between the bunk beds and the lavatory with one foot up on the commode. Her jeans are carelessly hung on the top of the bathroom door, with her shirt, panties, and bra hanging on the doorknob. She sure's not neat when roughing it.

There are bobby pins held between her neat white teeth, and her arms are lifted in graceful attention to her hair. It's a pleasant sight to observe as Gemini's putting her long hair in a tight bun, her breasts lifted in a perfect pose—up and pointing out—just pleading for you to give them some attention. You reach out to palm the lovely beauties with one hand, and turned on by Gemini looking like a Toulouse-Lautrec drawing with her leg up, vulva exposed, you encompass it with your other hand.

Continuing her toilet, she begins a sensuous rotation motion. With each voluptuous roll of her hips you slide your hand closer and closer to her feathery mound, until, without realizing it yourself, you're briskly rubbing her nipples and fondling her clitoris to the same rhythm. Gemini doesn't stop when her hair's complete. She just stands there grinding that lovely abdomen and now developing a hips-under-and-up-bump, grabbing your fingers as if by some unseen magnet hidden deep within her. Faster and faster she moves, until she braces herself against the door and forces your fingers deep inside her. Done now, she turns with loving gratitude to you, satisfaction shining in her eyes.

Coitus

All concern and attention are now on you; she's busy unbuttoning your favorite cotton fishing shirt and helping you remove it. Your erection finds relief as she yanks your denims brusquely from your legs. The bottom bunk is really too small for two people, but Gemini has the answer. First she settles you comfortably, then she kneels on the floor next to the bed and takes your penis in her mouth. She doesn't use fellatio to bring you to orgasm, she just tantalizes you to the peak of sensation. She contents herself with tracing imaginary designs on your belly while you get yourself under control. This start-and-stop pattern continues until you warn her that she's got you so excited you're going to explode right in her lovely mouth. She says go right ahead, and you do. The action isn't over, however.

Now she climbs in the bunk and positions herself directly over your once-again-erect penis. Slowly she lowers herself onto your ramrod-stiff organ. Then, just as slowly, she raises herself off your pole, but not far enough to lose contact. This action is repeated at an ever-quickening pace until you're sure the camper is going to rock onto its side. Even if the camper did tilt, you'd never notice, because by now both you and she are in the middle of a fantastic orgasm. This Gemini girl has just proved herself to be all woman. And remember, this is just the first few hours of your long weekend together.

Post-coitus

The next few hours bring needed rest. One bunk really not large enough for two, she beds down in the bunk next to you. She's flexible enough to know that only a good sleep can set you both up for a repeat, demand performance.

Five A.M. is early in anyone's book. But there she is, outside the camper, looking spic and span in a fresh shirt, her jeans belted with an Indian beaded affair. Watching her trying to brew coffee and prepare oatmeal in a frying pan causes an amused smile. How can this Gemini girl, as bright as quicksilver, do a foolish thing like that? But ... that's Gemini. You never know what daring, delicious, or silly thing she'll do next.

She greets you like a long-lost friend, as awake and with-it as if it were high noon instead of the crack of dawn.

Breakfasted, sweatered against the morning chill, and properly geared, you board your rowboat. Off you go into a great unknown adventure. The simplest fishing expedition is something special with a Gemini.

CANCER (June 22–July 21)

The Cancer Man

Recognition

Cancer men come in two decided types. Usually of average height, one may have a large, rather square-shaped face with a broad and muscular body, while another Cancer male may be very slim, with an equally slender face. These diversifications in physique make it difficult to pinpoint a Cancer male, but the trick is to spot him by concentrating on facial characteristics—a pronounced forehead, eyebrows most always paler than his hair, and small well-shaped ears.

His eyes will be large and either light blue or gray to hazel, with curly, long eyelashes. His nose is small, sometimes slightly turned up, with wide nostrils. The lips will be full and sensual.

Home is of the essence for the Moonchild, as if the motto "home sweet home" had been created for him especially. No other sign enjoys home and hearth like the Cancerian, because he has an innate need to be safe and protected within his own private circle. If he's really loved and is assured of this fact with consistency, he will be the happiest man around. His personality contains a natural ability to investigate matters, to view all angles of a situation. Not long in figuring it out, he seems to sense the solution without being helped or told.

This personality trait is reflected in his attitude toward clothes. He sticks to old things, and won't spend too much money, because he's tough when it comes to finances. He can't see foolish spending. This frugality shows in his clinging to old shirts and trousers, because to the Cancerian, if it's old then it's got to be valuable. Ancient tennis shoes or a high-school gym shirt is a must for the Cancerian guy, and when it comes to colors, they're largely of the earth—rust, green, brown, sienna—living woodsy colors.

Shaving lotion is very unimportant to this man. He'll go along with something manly like Old Spice or sandalwood. Bath accessories are negligible, but his two showers are a one hundred percent must as part of a fetish for cleanliness.

Jewelry is not a big item in his life. It doesn't go far or mean much to the Cancerian male. He might be intrigued into wearing a neck chain with his sign, the crab, on it. Or because his psychic ability is high, he might unbend a little and wear an occult medallion, but that's about it.

He's comic while fishing, because he'll drag out his oldest hat, loaded with hooks and feathers, and wear it at a jaunty "Barrymore" angle. A very funny man, this one. Even if not in show business, he's likely to be the center of attraction, never carrying on wildly, but amusing people with his dry sense of humor.

His humor, however, might mislead those around him, and the comedy-tragedy mask of the theater could be his trademark. He indulges in sadness—for himself and others, dramatically imagining the worst. Then, back he bounces; self-preservation comes first. He's truly content when he's with those he loves and is reassured of their affection for him.

When really hurt, he'll disappear into his shell, likely to cry and not be ashamed of it. This man craves harmony, and he's usually not the one to start an argument or create an unpleasant situation. If you're sharp with him, he'll retreat immediately, maybe taking a day or two to pull out of one of his depressed moods. He can never get enough love. He's intensely loyal, and if you exhibit your love, whether it's comedy or tragedy time, he'll be the sweetest man in the world.

The Cancerian is helpful to others, interested in their problems, and if he can help, he will. He probably won't offer, but if he's appealed to, he'll respond willingly. His face is an open book when he wants it to be that way, reacting to all you tell him about yourself, but he'll rarely talk about *his* innermost feelings. He's the sort to work them out himself. He has a tendency to daydream even while he's working in his slow but persistent manner, imagining a beautiful garden filled with spring flowers, a strictly private world. Who's there? Just him and his love of that moment.

It's a major crime to the Cancerian to waste food. "Waste not, want not" is his credo. His solution to your problems, whether you're sick, worried, or just plain tired, is to *eat*. He's a great chef usually, but dining isn't just a matter of sitting at the table. Breaking bread is a spiritual meeting of minds, one of the most important acts of living. A tremendous need for home and family is reflected in his love of holiday gatherings of the clan or anniversary and birthday celebrations.

The many-faceted Moonchild has a fantastic memory. He can astound you with pertinent facts of great consequence and amaze you with the trivia he recalls. Remembering telephone numbers, street addresses, Social Security or Army serial numbers is another of his feats.

Where to Find Him

Since environment and atmosphere are important to the Cancerian male's outlook and attitude, you'll find him in a lively place with pleasant people. Any sort of pressure outside of business turns him off, because he's really a gentle spirit when not involved with his job. He'll do a fine job no matter what it is, but he has to be treated nicely. If there's a family business, he'll likely be a part of it. He's not only tied to mom's apron strings, he's tied to the entire family. This doesn't mean he can't function without advice and consent—it's strictly an emotional fusing.

Many Cancerians are fine actors and excellent mimics. Their depth of feeling and understanding moves them creatively and allows full exhibition of emotions. Many Shakespearean tragedians have been Cancerians, too. They're versatile workers, make excellent chefs, and due to their extraordinary psychic ability, can be good detectives. Cancer males do their own thing, always searching for the beautiful and interesting. They love rummaging through antique shops, and although not interested mechanically in old classic cars, may very well be collectors of them. The old is always valuable, and they're strongly drawn to things of the past.

Because of their financial frugality, they make fine merchants and are the best "deal makers" around. The word "merchant" in Moonchild's vocabulary is more than just a candy store with a ten- and a fifteen-cent chocolate bar for sale. The concept is "buy for one dollar and sell for two dollars," and that goes into the millions.

Cancer males are some of the most successful entrepreneurs in the world. They have a way of getting the best of a bargain or coming out on top in any business situation. Their crablike manner in evading issues until they're ready to deal with them or their ability to dance around the periphery of a sticky point until the moment is ripe is something of genius.

In earlier times, when world trade was first born, you can be sure it was a Cancerian with whom Marco Polo made his deals for the import-export phase. Just remember, you can't come up with a winner haggling with him. Your only chance for success is to play it his way on a deal, or pull his own tactics and retreat. He's a frustrating, fabulous financier.

Primary Move

Because he's such an open sort socially, he'll enjoy your laughing at his jokes. The Cancerian learns from life's experience, so that perhaps something "new" like you in his life may be suspect for a while. Play it by ear, enjoy him from moment to moment, sort of inching your way into his heart. He's absolutely impossible where his time is concerned, fitting seven or eight items into a two-hour period that would normally take four. It's not that he's contemptuous of others' time when he keeps them waiting for appointments twenty or thirty minutes, it's just there aren't enough hours in a day to "wheel and deal."

Since he's a nut for antiques, tell him about some shop you've found, maybe thirty miles away, and use your car. He'll enjoy sitting back and letting his mind wander on the many situations he has pending. In fact, he'll leap at the opportunity, and will be perceptive enough to realize that you recognize his need for removal from the hustle-bustle of his busy days.

Do your homework on antiques first, though, because you can't fool a Cancer guy when it comes to the cut of glass, the year a fine cupboard was hand-crafted, or the value of antique jewelry. Browse with him all day long, because this sort of activity relaxes him and puts his mind at ease.

After this antique prowling, tell him you know of a quaint restaurant nearby with a fireplace. His choices food-wise are well-rounded and may range from a beef stew, thick with

The Lovers' Guide to Sensuous Astrology 55

meat and hearty vegetables and potatoes, to seafood, which is one of his favorites. He loves all kinds of fish, crabs, or clams. And when it comes to dessert, he relishes Key lime or lemon-meringue pie. You'll be treated like a child when you dine with a Cancerian. So, please, don't leave anything on your plate!

Although the environment of home is more important to him than food, don't starve him; and even if you don't visit a friend or can't find a quaint place to dine, take him home and scramble some eggs. It'll go just as well.

Once settled in, direct the dining conversation toward the occult or the latest book you've read on transcendental meditation or psychic developments behind the Iron Curtain. Mystery excites him, and the occult challenges his mental agility. If you feel he's in his dream garden, shake the garden gate a bit. The hinges are well-oiled. Enter smiling and walk with your hand in his.

If he suddenly looks at his watch and realizes he's thirty-five minutes late for a business appointment, try to keep disappointment from spoiling the afternoon. The odds are one hundred to one he's not fabricating an appointment. There's no doubt he's using his leisure days to cement a business situation—he's always the merchant.

There'll be other opportunities, and if they don't come fast enough, you'll invent them.

Pre-coitus

He's the boss, big brother, and father of all he surveys. He's a loving, giving, generally wealthy, frugal, home-loving, energetic, hard-working success. The crab, representative of his sign of the zodiac, is a misnomer. "Moonchild" is more apropos. A touch of silver moonbeam streaks his hair; his laugh is hearty. His outward self seems cool, his interior private—hidden seas and craters. Earthy jokes and unworldly visions make him a constant question mark ... in opposition to logical understanding. He's hard to figure out. Attuned physically to all things, he requires the strong ties of home and the family unit.

But this is what you want. All of him. His dynamite being. His sensuous loving, his charming gifts of words and phrases. You think: "Maybe some of it will rub off on me!" Well, give it a try!

The best approach is to meet the love master in his lair,

his castle of accomplishment, his office—usually decorated with heavy pieces of furniture complementing his masculinity, and scattered with mementos from friends and family. He rules his world from the $650 desk chair. Padded, but not too soft; high back, but not such that it dwarfs his physique; and always on casters, to facilitate his moves behind the many buttons on private boxes and ringing telephones. An oiled-spring chair expertly manfactured so that with a click of the wrist he can arrange a reclining position for a ten-minute catnap, which is as refreshing to him as an hour or two to some others.

If you need help, he's the one to see. It's an excellent ploy to use to get to know him better. The Cancer man always has a hand extended to guide you to your destination. No matter how busy his day, and it's usually madness—committee meetings, in-house staff conferences, stock-market reports, and tons of reading—he'll clear away a place in the middle of bedlam to see you. An appointment is a necessity, but since you met him first at one of the many charitable affairs he attends frequently, it's easy to arrange. He'll remember your name when you call, and if any electricity sparked between you, he'll clear his desk the day of your phone call.

After a cordial greeting, you're sitting across his expansive desk, smiling, alert to his merest nuance of mood. He likes this. The Moonchild likes it when you react in accordance with his manner and feeling of the moment. You've dreamed up an impossible scheme to present to him for this meeting, and find he's talking about anything and everything from ancient mythology to modern cybernetics. Your comments amuse and satisfy him that you have a marvelous mind. Moonchild is even more appreciative. Then, without preamble, out of nowhere, you hear him say, "Tell me about yourself." You try to prevent a guilty grin appearing on your face, and think to yourself, "If he only knew, I'd like to bed him, and that's why I'm here!" But he does know! Supersensitive to most people, he can almost read your mind. Why do you think he's such a success? He uses his inborn psychic facility to read and psyche out those he deals with, even you.

Coitus

You start to explain, and as you go into your phony song and dance about this ridiculous plan you're nurturing, he

The Lovers' Guide to Sensuous Astrology   57

leaves his chair and flicks the gold-filled locks on two doors. Nonchalantly walking to the great expanse of windows in his office, he draws the draperies. On the way back to his chair, he stops a moment, places his hand on your shoulder, squeezes it, and with his other arm, helps you from your side of the desk to his. You're now engulfed in his desk chair, which seems the size of a settee. His lap is comfortable, and you know that mission's almost accomplished. But, "One more thing, darling," he whispers. Buzzing his secretary, he announces he wants no calls or disturbances until he rings her again. Faithful old gray mare out there is sure he's about to pull another coup, buying up the other half of the state of Nevada perhaps!

It's nice being snug in his arms. Cancer man is an aggressive lover, and your worst fears are over. You're ready to move, but he's way ahead of you. Murmuring in your ear that he has exactly thirty minutes to devote to this dalliance, he works swiftly to untie the knot in his tie, disengages the watch from his wrist, indicating to you to hop off his lap and untie his shoelaces ... which you do, caught by surprise at the terse command. You really hadn't planned it this way, but ... he did.

In his stocking feet now, he's busily clearing his conference-size desk of all papers. As he sorts them carefully in little piles on the credenza behind the desk, he points you to his executive rest room, shower stall and all, to remove your clothes and leave them in there.

Still in shock at the fast pace, you acquiesce. Upon returning to his office you find a veritable harem bed on top of his desk. Pillows from the sofa stacked around, overhead lights out, with just the dim glow of painting exhibit lights filling the room with a dreamlike, out-of-space Moonchild quality.

Moonchild embraces you, a bear hug of affection. Kisses you with friendly attention on each cheek, then lifts your arms and nuzzles his nose there, taking tiny bites at the sides of each breast, ignoring the nipples. Walking backwards with you in his arms, he puts his buttocks on the edge of the desk. He pulls you toward him between spread-eagled legs, inserting his penis between your thighs. You're still unable to fathom this curious Cancer man. But don't try, he's got his outline set up far in advance. Now you're sure what you thought about him is true. It's not quantity with Cancer, but the best of quality.

You didn't notice that as he held you closely, moving his

penis in a slow iambic meter between your thighs, he glanced at the large sculptured clock over his door. Fifteen minutes to go!

Gracefully and with the same nonchalance he showed earlier, he lifts you bodily to the desk, encircles you with pillows, but your body feels just the hard wood of his desk beneath. Deftly and with businesslike precision he lifts your hips and places a pillow under your derriere. Meanwhile, although your body is pulsing with unbelievable sexual stimulation, he's achieved this by neither touching your erect nipples nor your equally excited clitoris. That nibble or two under your arm was too fast to count. Patience, for now is the grand opening. He's kneeling between your legs, his hard log ready to put in the fire. Grasping your hips, instead of penetrating himself, he brings both your legs across his chest, your feet resting on his shoulders, and draws you onto his penis. Ohhhh! Wondrous, curious, scintillating Cancer!

Then he moves, and it's quality. Each thrust a masterpiece. No timid motions for him. Just . . . take this . . . and this . . . and that . . . and . . . .

Somewhere in the velvet blackness of your mind, lost in spinning space with your Moonchild, you hear a clock chime three. As if on cue, your Cancer man has stopped his poignant pushing and is now pressing your bottom and thighs closer to his body. You feel the shuddering, spastic movement of his entire frame as he orgasms.

Post-coitus

It seems that not a moment passes but he's extricated his diminished penis and is wiping it with tissues. He's off the desk in a flash and stage-whispers to you to put the pillows back on the sofa.

Your recovery is slower, but as you stir, you see a shirttail enter the john. By the time the pillows are back in place, he's out of the bathroom and pointing for you to go there and dress. The whole episode was like an Alice in Wonderland meeting! You quickly french-bathe, dress, touch up your makeup, and comb your hair. Almost giggling aloud, you think, "And I was going to seduce him!"

As you open the door to return to the office, it's filled with late-afternoon sunlight, papers once again stacked on his desk, and he's on the phone berating some poor soul about selling short too soon.

Amazement is the only word you can summon up, and that's it. That's how it is with the Cancer male. He places the receiver in the cradle of the telephone, immediately rises, walks you to the door while pecking somewhere in the vicinity of your cheek, and says, "I'll call you."

Next thing you know, you're smiling woodenly at his secretary and practically stumble blindly to the elevator. No, it'll never really be any different. Perhaps not in his office. Perhaps somewhere else. Perhaps a whole evening or a weekend, but basically you're scheduled in. It's worth it, because it's quality with the Cancer man, unsurpassed quality.

The Cancer Woman

Recognition

"Baby face, you've got the cutest little baby face." The theme song of the Cancer woman. But there's another side, too.

Cancer females usually have a predominantly round or lunar-looking physiognomy, or it may be a bit square, but never sharp. The eyes are set wide apart beneath a very full forehead, and the look in those eyes is nothing short of luminous. Luckily for Moonchildren, the face has a tendency to stay young and beautiful throughout life.

The Cancer gal has a way of looking at you with eyes full of innocence, revealing the secret of her entire being. The look of love is quite definitely in this lady's eyes. Prone to show hurt, she may dissolve in tears, which she can't successfully hide.

Her nose is usually full, with a wide bridge and a tendency to turn piquantly skyward. She likes to rub it while she's thinking.

She's like a warm and loving cherub, with full, wide lips and a very sensual look overall. Those full lips demand subtle color from the Cancer female, and she has to watch out for inborn allergy to some cosmetics. Her artistic fingertips will blend rouge skillfully, utilizing a peach tone if she isn't tan, but getting rambunctious once in a while and daring a cherry red. Since her eyes are her most outstanding feature, she goes in for heavy eye makeup and false eyelashes, but has the talent to make it look good.

Her lustrous hair ranges in tones from a light brown to a dark brunette, but usually not black. The texture is soft, but her hair is thick and usually extremely wavy, with little tendrils escaping her coiffure.

This gal is small, rarely topping five-feet-four. She'll have petite bone structure, a long, slender neck, and very broad shoulders to support the voluptuous bosom.

She walks at a slow pace, not striding, but moving casually, with a feminine grace. She strolls, undeterminedly, but with mincing steps. The rocking rhythm to her gait is a mark of the excellent dancer.

The Cancer woman must watch her weight. She's an excellent cook and loves to taste the results of her culinary efforts. No can openers around her kitchen. She enjoys the creativity of cooking, and even an ordinary roast can become a masterpiece. No gooey desserts; just give her an angel cake, pound cake, or lady fingers, and it'll suffice.

There's usually a distant look in her expression, as if she were wandering alone in her own special dream world. Cancer females can be singled out by the ethereal quality they exude while in motion. Personally they are extremely changeable, very sensitive, and emotionally on a roller coaster, with mercurial switches in mood and temper.

Her well-shaped legs are not long; the upper arms are full, soft, and feminine, with the lower portion ending in very thin, delicate wrists. Her fingers may be a variety of lengths; the look is small, capable. This gal has a built-in artistic touch.

As to clothes, if it's old, it's good. She'll wear things for comfort, relaxing in a Mickey Mouse T-shirt with frayed jeans. She really enjoys odd combinations of colors—red and pink, emerald with turquoise, Indian prints and brilliant Egyptian coloring.

She's a family girl with great affection for ancestry. One side of this tiny personality is gone on heirloom cameo brooches and little antique jeweled pins. Then, on the opposite side of the scale, exotic earrings and full, heavy Aztec ornaments.

Her perfume is surprisingly heavy for so small a woman. She adores the mysterious scents of light incense or the odor of orange or strawberry.

Drinking is a question mark with the Cancer woman. She can appreciate a boozeless concoction and often prefers it. She does enjoy sweet-flavored liqueurs after dinner or over her desserts. "Ladies' drinks," like Alexanders or Pink Ladies, in tall, thin-stemmed glasses, are a delight. Her drinking is decidedly limited, and she'd never be that loud drunk you regret meeting.

Where to Find Her

When visiting a nursery school, nine times out of ten the little ladies you'll meet will be Cancers, taking care of four-years to five-year-olds or feeding and changing babies. They make excellent teachers and nurses because of their compassionate makeup. If you're in for a medical checkup, the lady under that cute little tipped-up hat might well be the lady you're seeking. Moonchildren make excellent doctors, too, especially in the field of gynecology and pediatrics.

Attend concerts if you want to spot her. She's an avid fan of the symphony and opera and might herself study music. She has very facile and creative hands and could play the harpsichord, an instrument from the past. It engenders her love of music as well as satisfying her love of antiquity. Poetry, short stories, and vignettes also find this sign in ascendancy, able to describe their innermost feelings with ease and beauty of expression.

Although the Cancer's sensitive skin would seem to belie this, a good percentage of the girls lounging around a pool are Cancers. They are mermaids, not lounge lizards, female variety. They love to expose their bodies attractively in expensive bikinis. They shine in a well-fitting and revealing bathing suit. Perhaps this love of water relates to their crab sign.

Lounging, yes. But most often no strenuous exercise for these chicks. No racing, skiing, tennis, or any overly active sport finds them among the fans. But they dig the sauna, just sitting and letting the skin moisten.

Classic ballet, as well as the contemporary frug, satisfies

her love of dancing—in the local pub, on stage, or as the prima ballerina in a fine company.

In an office situation, Cancer girls make fantastic and loyal secretaries because of their determination and dependability. Not desirous of being leaders, they'll give their all for the boss (if he deserves it). Technically, they are expert even if they dream along with their routine duties. So, check secretaries, receptionists, and even dental technicians, and you may strike Cancer gold.

The lady is very much affected by what's happening *now* and whether what's happening is good for her or whether it endangers her security. If it does, she'll retreat rather than fight. At a party, you'll most likely spot her in the corner of an oversized sofa talking with one or two people, enjoying conversation about the psychic and occult. She has the habit of making knowledgeable statements without really knowing all the details about the subject of discussion. She's quite perceptive, and she'll study your face, not quizzically, but with those eyes penetrating your very soul.

Primary Move

The Moonchild has a slightly wistful, fey quality about her. It's not so much a dreamy look, but rather that she lives or seems to live in a rainbow bubble. She's so home- and family-oriented that an invitation to your apartment is the essence of good taste. She'll never believe you have surreptitious motives.

Serve her a delightful, carefully prepared meal. Take special care not only with the cuisine but with your silver, dishes, and the general decor of your table. Make it elegant. Have red wine or chilled champagne awaiting her. Place flowers on the table in a crystal bowl. The Cancerian woman loves bright, shiny objects. For example, a cut-glass cigarette box, or a silvered mirror ball on an antique stand, even if inexpensive.

A clear, brightly shining glass pitcher filled with clinking ice cubes and water will catch her eye and delight her senses. Accessories like this in the room will give her a secure feeling. She admires cleanliness and neatness, so make sure both you and your apartment are sparkling.

Dress casually, but please her sense of good grooming. Have your slacks knife-creased, sport shirt crisp-looking, shoes shined, topped off with a handsome sweater. This attire

The Lovers' Guide to Sensuous Astrology 63

appeals to her. In short, whether you're the male-model type, handsome and virile-looking, or not, wear an outdoorsy scent exuding an air of masculine protectiveness. You can bet she'll be having pipe dreams of moving the stereo from here to there and rearranging the pictures in your living room.

Show your concern for her health, comfort, and pleasure. Be attentive to details with this woman, in order to encourage trust and remove her inhibitions. Baby her. The more you do it, the better she likes it. Romantic compliments flatter her. If you want to tell her that she has a ravishing figure, or lovely eyes, by all means do so. She likes this approach. Make those compliments sincere; she can't cope with the feeling she's being toyed with. You must impart to her by all you say and do that she's a special person and that you're especially delighted she's a part of your world.

Take it slow and step-by-step with the Cancerian. Be warm, friendly, and complimentary, but don't mistake the last-named for flattery. She'll tag you because of her extremely astute perception.

Start by telling her how lovely her hair looks. No need to play games. Be simple and direct in your approach, because later on she'll be the one who'll be frivolous and tricky.

When you're ready to serve dinner, let her decide whether or not she wants a cocktail. Encourage her to talk about family reminiscences. Then lead in gently to compliments about her figure and what a gentle, loving parent she'd be. Whatever else may be true about a Cancer girl, the home is her world.

The salad course might give you cause to mention her artistic hands, and you'll sense her melting under your spell. Make her feel needed, wanted, and tell her how pleased you are to meet a girl as special as she is. She'll react, no doubt at all!

Touch her hand, and if she pulls away, know that she really doesn't want to, but that she's basically shy. You're breaking down barriers, and once you decide you want to win her, and accomplish this feat, she's yours—and I mean *yours!* And you are *hers!*

The crab syndrome comes in here, for she clings like a devil, loves you, warms you, overprotects you. This is an involvement. No "Wham-bam, thank-you, ma'am" for her.

After dinner she's going to offer to do the dishes. Let her. After all, the kitchen's the heart of the home—how familiar and intimate she'll feel.

Pre-coitus

Keep the lights dim. Use orange or red bulbs in a couple of your lamps. You'll see how quickly she reacts to the sentimental warmth of this atmosphere.

Head her toward a comfortable chair and sit at her feet, smoking a pipe perhaps, and while reminiscing about the meal and her charming chatter, take off her shoes and start massaging her feet. Just rub them slowly, letting your fingers go in and out of the toes. Massage each little toe individually, as if she were a child and you were playing a bedtime game with her (and aren't you?). Then massage her instep, first kneading your fingers in a very slow, deep massage; then quicken the pace. Of course, what you're doing is giving her a foreshadowing of what's to come. Now to the lower part of her calf, all the while talking about other things, like "Have you ever read Thoreau?" and "Did you hear the latest recording by the London Philharmonic?" Most Cancerian women are very involved in music. Anything and everything that's related to the arts is of special interest.

As you slowly massage her calf, doing it properly and not too sensually, casually suggest she remove her stockings simply because it would be easier for you. She'll accept this rationale, because by now she wants to be with you as much as you want her to be.

She'll probably leave the room to take off her pantyhose. When she comes back, rearrange your position on the floor and take her hand and guide her to sit beside you. As she comfies down and nestles in, let your fingers run up her inner thigh to stimulate her, then tease, stop. Go back to her other foot and begin again. This is a marvelous way to turn on the Cancerian woman.

At first it's hard for her to disrobe completely, but as you continue your massage from foot to calf to thigh, after a couple of times you will manage to obtain her cooperation. Surely but gently, stroke her legs, each time reaching nearer and nearer, and finally let your fingers slip right up to the edge of the lips of the vagina, then stop. Although you know she's ready for conquest, play it cool. Stand up, take off your sweater, and open your shirt. By this time it won't offend her; she'll welcome the progress. Help her up from the floor. As you do so, go behind her and start massaging the muscles around her neck. Touch her neck, then her shoulders, voluptuously. Breathe a little harder, foreshadow again, because now you make your first obvious move.

Coitus

Unzip or unbutton her blouse or dress. Reach for her breasts; bring them out into the open. Touch her nipple and aureole. As you do this, talk about how wonderfully hard and erect her cocoa-brown nipples are, how they miraculously respond to your touch like two trained puppies. Walk in front of her, bend down, and put one excited nipple in your mouth. Suck it. Concentrate on actually sucking the nipple, as if you were a baby, gently, first hunting for the nipple. Then grab it gruffly with your lips. More firmly now, suck away. This is what the Cancerian woman loves. Remember, she's very home- and family-oriented. Lovemaking of this nature is very important.

Put your hand on her shoulder and her other nipple in your mouth, shaping your mouth like a fish's, anxious to snatch the delicate bait. Suck this breast. She can multi-orgasm from sex play like this. Needless to say, both of you will now be in a state of anxious anticipation for further and deeper stimulation.

Lift her gently, murmuring how petite and lightweight she is as you carry the Moonchild in your arms to the bedroom. She adores being babied.

There is one very important item to remember. Be positive that the bedroom is neat. The size of the room doesn't matter, nor whether the bed is comfortable, as long as you're certain everything is clean and neat. Make sure there are no loose hairpins or female hair clips around, nothing belonging to another woman. You can be confident if she sees traces of another girl, it's total turn-off and goodnight. It's the mood you create with a Cancerian woman, the mood of home, family, and involvement.

After you have tenderly placed her on your bed and plumped the pillows comfortably under her head, sit down on the bed beside her. Place your arm around her waist as you touch her hesitantly, the way you would a precious china doll. Undress her, lovingly but not sexually, and let your fingers glide over her body.

Bring a cold glass of white wine to her and hold it between her breasts as you sip, cushioning your face against those ripe peaches. Lift the glass to her mouth and let her sip it too. Then lightly dip your fingers in the wine, touching her nipples with the moisture, lining her pale-gold aureoles. Lap it off. Again dip your fingers into the wine and anoint the lips of her vagina, then let your tongue delicately curl around each drop, sometimes darting deep within the honeyed cleft. Her clitoris will become a diminutive steeple. Climb the steeple with your fingers and explore its heights.

The pace should be slow and sure. A Cancerian woman blossoms like a flower when you extend your foreplay. By now you're on the bed beside her. Move her face to see your penis, stiff now with longing for her. Seeing this physical display in response to her loveliness, she's ready to give herself, and you're in for a complete and total treat, because she'll do all under the sun to please you. The way she's made, it's not as important to her to have an orgasm as it is to feel she's making you happy.

As she readies to make a move, encourage her by whispering loving words. She's not overly aggressive, so if she wants to nibble your back or bite your shoulders, reassure her. Then, as if you just cannot resist any longer, enfold her in your arms and stop talking.

Mount her carefully—she's a little person; then, with groans of delight, enter her. Some of the zodiac signs like complete silence, but not the Cancerian. No conversation, but she loves sounds of contentment and heavy, deep breathing and sighs.

Now that your penis is in the vagina, withdraw, insert, withdraw, insert again, aiming it first far left in the canal, then far right, then right up the middle.

Purr like a tomcat, growl deep in your throat like a giant Great Dane. With all these sound effects, she'll know she's bringing much joy to you. Slow. Go slow. She'll urge you on when she's ready to have you pick up the tempo. It's now!

The Moonchild will probably have so many orgasms previous to coitus that maintaining your equilibrium won't be difficult. The act, though not too swift, does not have to be an endurance test. The sensitivity you exhibit during the final moments—holding her closely and hushing her panting mouth with kisses—is of great importance.

Post-coitus

If you are too abrupt after copulating, it would totally destroy the new relationship. You must be very tender, very quiet with her now. If you see her crying, don't be alarmed; those tears are probably tears of joy. Cancerian woman cries easily; she cries out of delight, out of exquisite pain; she has a very wholesome attitude toward sex.

Assuring her of your great pleasure in sharing her gorgeous body and of the happiness in being close will make it all seem very worthwhile to her. There's always that little guilty flicker of conscience that enters with the Moonchild, denying her the full pleasure of the experience. It would have been much more to her liking if there were a ring, third finger, left hand!

So, by the way, watch yourself, you could really fall for her, and hard. Moonchildren make fantastic wives and have a way with men, making marriage the only answer to really living. So, in your relationship with a Cancerian woman, always keep in mind that you might be caught!

LEO (July 22–August 21)

The Leo Man

Recognition

The Leo man! This is the progenitor of the race, the noble monarch of his kingdom, ruler of everybody and everything! You'll know it, too, by his large head, easily held on a full, round neck, leonine, frank, and forceful like the autocrat he is. On the top of that big head you'll find curly hair, slightly unmanageable, and usually light in color.

This king of the jungle has a fair, ruddy, or florid complexion and a face that's always alive and laughing, a typical example of *joie de vivre*. His more-often-than-not blue eyes sparkle with a joke or a glint scarcely hidden there.

His chin will generally be round, but quite definite, never soft or saggy. As he grows older, however, his cheeks sometimes sag, and he'll take on more and more the look of Leo the Lion. He has a full lower lip, and his nose is prominent but well-proportioned and impressive, with that Leo upper lip jutting out right under the nose.

The Leo man has a way of carrying himself and extending his personality to make those around him feel alive even if they're depressed. He's usually medium to tall, with big, broad shoulders, a strong back, and an ample chest held very high. His hips are very narrow, and his legs, while a bit thin, with bony knees, don't detract from the overall look. Who really cares about his legs when you're facing one of the most temperately dispositioned, kind-hearted persons in the zodiac?

The Lovers' Guide to Sensuous Astrology 69

The Leo is outspoken and expends his energy lavishly, but he's also sympathetic and always carries with him a feeling of optimism, of great hope and faith in himself and in humanity. He'll turn on when others express their interest in him. He has a fanatic desire for power, loves to be in command, sort of a kindly dictator, but he'll achieve his aims gently, with no malice or hatred ever in the process.

Disagreements uncork his high-strung temperament, and he's quick to anger. But his temper passes like a summer squall, the calm bringing his cheerful self back to the fore.

The "King" exhibits his very being by wearing vibrant colors, which he feels add to the wonder of being alive and being a Leo. He wears reds, golds, and has the knack for combining just the right colors to create a dazzling effect. It's not necessarily innate good taste on his part; it's just that the colors he likes blend well together. He'll go for colorful and unique bathing suits, like a full one-piece job instead of trunks. If he's up north, he'll affect a fur coat and fur hat; and he'll look sensational!

If he's the affluent sort, he'll splurge on formal outfits in the very latest style, the newest cut in evening shirts, with lace cuffs and frilly jabots, and no one will kid him about it, because his appearance is commanding and kingly. He's attracted to tweeds, even morning clothes and toppers if he's in the proper business or has an afternoon formal. At home it's satin bathrobes in rich colors for him, smoking jackets of brocade, colorful underwear. In short, more clothes than he'll ever be able to wear. His socks will be of exquisite quality, and you won't see them falling down around his ankles, either.

In the jewelry line, he favors diamonds and rubies or cat's-eyes because of their golden stare. His jewelry will be the real McCoy, a good ring or two and watches of gold or platinum.

Food to him is an experience, so like sex and most of his tastes, it's got to be the best. Dining to the Leo is equated with a meeting of the minds . . . and eventually, bodies. He's not the ready-made-hamburger or hot-dog type, because he favors the best restaurants in the world, fine music, excellent service, and appropriate lighting.

He digs such oddball seasoning as rosemary and saffron, curry, lemon, pepper, dill, and chives. He'll go for walnuts in his vegetables, rice with saffron, and wants the "whole thing"—from soup to nuts. The food itself can be almost anything, but it has to be prepared with style and possess an identity sporting a subtle flavor or a very spicy one, nothing in between, mundane, or flat. Give it character and excitement, and you've got an enthusiastic diner.

The Leo man hates eating alone and might very well skip a meal or two rather than dine by himself, because he communicates while he dines, often reaching a sensuous level within himself. He likes all the elaborate fixings, too—candles, crystal, silver, china, napkins, and always a lavish, showy dessert, like baked Alaska or the various flambéd specialties.

He prefers champagne or cognac to hard liquor, being a believer in life's good things, settling only for the highest ideals of living, the most perfect way to enjoy his exciting life.

Where to Find Him

This king of the world could be a pilot, because he's got to be the master of his environment. He's the type who glories in doing for others, and even with heavy responsibilities in a business world, you'll find him involved in charitable works, fund-raising activities. Not just a philanthropist, but a physical activist in worthy causes. He has many friends, which means many requests, and if they're viable, you'll never hear this man saying no.

There's hardly anything in the world of sports he doesn't like to do, and because he enjoys battling the elements, boating and deep-sea fishing especially appeal to him. If he's office-bound, he'll still find time for an hour at the gym, not just to work out, but to engage a sparring partner or take his energy out on the punching bag.

This man is ready at all times to shoulder responsibility, and he's tops at providing a home for his family. He makes a wonderful master of ceremonies, because his humorous side is highly appealing. He's really a pied piper, because even if you disagree with him, you've sort of got to laugh along with him.

The Leo is one of the few who can blow his own horn and make people love him for it. Many of them are entrepreneurs, the go-between in realty, mortgage, or banking deals. They make fine diplomats, and if moneyed, will live up to their income, in lavishly decorated homes.

If he's not on the wealthy side, he'll still put more into his home or apartment than he can afford, and will scrimp on his clothes budget in order to live nicely.

His hobbies and avocations are securely in the realm of helping other people, and the wealthy among his tribe can usually be found carrying that attribute to the limit through their talent for raising money to support their philanthropic causes.

Primary Move

Love with a capital "L" is a must in the life of a Leo man. Without love he really can't survive, so he's always looking and always open to that essential commodity. He needs desperately to feel he's wanted, and needs to know you can accept and enjoy his love, not only through appreciation but by a show of total love on your part.

Don't forget, no one exists but the King. Be a delightful and very loving lady with the Leo man. Try tossing a dinner party for a girlfriend, or maybe celebrate your mother's birthday or your father's retirement from business. Invite creative people, showy people, eccentric and glamorous characters, and by doing this you will be setting the scene like a stage, providing him with a perfect evening.

Have candles and bright lights, flowers, and if possible, hire someone to serve at the table. Above all, listen to his grandiose plans, because he's not just a talker, he's a doer, and he'll make those plans reality.

You can honestly and openly play up to the Leo man with your eyes, your mind, and your body. Praise him and tell him he's the greatest. Almost more than any other sign, the Leo is concerned with what you wear while dining, so lower the decolletage a bit, and *your* party will begin when the party's over!

Pre-coitus

The Leo man is temporarily sated. A sparkling evening, topped off by a cherry flambé and good hot coffee to fill his stomach ... and by partially exposed breasts providing food on which to feast his eyes.

You've set the scene well. Guests gone, lights extinguished, just candle-glow with friendly, flickering flames joining the restful, quiet atmosphere of the room. This represents the whole meaning of life to the Leo man. A sumptuous castle, gorgeous accouterments, good food well prepared, and a woman ready to run, trip, or fall at his command. The bared breasts are an extra bonus.

He's most protective of precious and expensive things, so suggesting you remove your lovely gown and make yourself comfortable may not be strictly a "come-on."

You'll think, "Hup-two-three-four, move on command," but you'll smile back benevolently at this thoughtful lion. Now's your chance to wear some seductive lounging robe, silvered and appliquéd with flowers in pinks and purples. If you're in a cold climate, a fur-trimmed robe pleases his sense of opulence.

Jacket removed, tie off, collar opened, cigar lit, he's buckling in for a long flight, destination not certain. Come back to the room doing a double twirl, with your robe buttoned only to the top of the thigh, exposing your lovely treat. Long, well-tapered legs stretching in and out of your luxurious garment, with your furry delight peeping out now and then, can entice your Leo lover to the heights of desire. His eyes are always searching for beautiful objects, and he *must* have them. No price is too high to pay, and he remains appreciative of the worth.

Unpin your coiffure in front of him and let the maze of confection-sweet hair tumble loosely. His leonine head will nod in appreciation as he beckons you to his side, unaware that your scheme for near-rape is close at hand.

Since you're so rapturously cozy and cheery in your glamorous housecoat, suggest he slip into a satin mandarin robe you picked up for your father on a recent trip. You won't have to draw pictures to let him know what you want. He can validate his air-flight ticket. He's sure that "uncertain destination" is now known.

While he's neatly placing his shirt on the back of a living-room chair and his hands are headed for his shoestrings, take a candlestick in each hand and bring it into milady's chamber. Hopefully, you saved pennies and made your playpen a comfortable and lovely bower in which to court the King of Lions, your Leo man.

Arrange yourself seductively on top of the satin comforter, draped like Godiva on the pillows, with only your hair flowing to cover your naughty but nice nudity. He arrives at the chamber door. As he stands there drinking in the lush sight of you, rearrange your body, as if making live pictures for him.

Sit up like a pinup girl, arms stretched behind you on the bed, one knee bent up. Separate your legs ever so slightly and move your shoulders to one side, then the other, briskly making your breasts agitate. He'll be spellbound by your loveliness.

Now you're a calendar girl. Up on your hands and knees, derriere toward him, peeking over your shoulder at your Leo man, smiling lewdly while your buttocks move rhythmically, inviting him to the bed. As he approaches, lie on your back; he doesn't need a navigator to fly him to your fetchingly extended arms. He's radared in for a landing on your softly paved runway. Flaps up, wheels down, he is!

He is lying beside you, breathing words of endearment in your ear. You feel his broadsword poking you in the belly, so proceed to show him what a loving subaltern you are.

The King enjoys the protocol and ceremony of all his endeavors. A silver tray, prepared earlier, carrying a crystal jar filled with thick honey-colored cream should cause him to wonder. Dip your fingers in the perfumed cream and very delicately and very, very slowly begin to anoint your Leo man's genital area. Starting a few inches below his navel, trail your fingers down to the base of his penis. Then very carefully coat every inch of his penis, paying special attention to and lingering over the head. Then work back, very gently stroking his testicles and the sensitive area behind them. Go back to his by now ramrod-stiff penis and grasp it at the base. Slide your hand up and down on his slippery shaft, slowly and gently at first, but then faster and faster. It won't be long before you feel the telltale throbbing in his penis that signals the start of his orgasm. He'll be delighted with you and your sophisticated and thrilling version of a hand-job.

To further heighten the effect of the King and his serving girl, leave the room briefly and return with a bowl of warm sudsy water, a washcloth, and a fluffy towel. Lather him up, clean him off thoroughly, and then gently dry him off. You can expect to be rewarded with a kiss for your attentions.

Remember, this is just the warm-up before the main event. Leo is already showing signs that he's ready for more action.

Coitus

He wants you to be aware of the more delicate areas of his lovemaking, so before he makes his move to enter you, he'll twist around and bury his face between your legs. Gently parting your nether lips, he'll probe with his tongue until he locates your clitoris, and then concentrate most of his efforts on that. Keeping his mouth glued to your excited pussy, he'll maneuver you around until you're in a comfortable position to take his penis in your mouth and do for him what he's doing (and doing so thrillingly) for you.

Leo man makes this project a long, drawn-out affair, first voraciously lapping, then gently nipping. His versatility with cunnilingus amazes you. The sensations reach their peak, and you both shudder in mutual orgasm.

Believe it or not, he isn't finished yet. Before you even get your breath back, Leo is astride you, and without any of the previous frills, his thrusts again bring you to an explosive orgasm.

Post-coitus

You've done it. You've succeeded in pleasing him in every possible way and fulfilling all his needs.

Propped up on four pillows, hands folded beneath his head, he'll ramble on and on about all the fabulous things he'll do for you, expensive clothes he'll buy for you, and the perfect days and nights he's planned for you. And he means it. Leo man is not one to talk in vain. Your night of love is a clincher. He's conjuring visions of villas on the Riviera, a flat in London, a townhouse in New York, for you . . . and him.

Yes, better forget your other attachments; this is the King, and he's decided you're to be his Queen.

The Leo Woman

Recognition

The most outstanding characteristics of the Leo woman are an aura of extreme vitality, a regal look, and a magnetism that exudes from every pore. This vitality and queenliness are what will capture you first. They are qualities she possesses more than does any other sign.

She holds her head high on a round columnlike, full neck. Her face is round, too, with wideawake eyes, always bright and alert, sometimes full of innocence. Even when tired or relaxing in her den, her eyes have that inner sparkle, and she herself always has that aura of royalty.

With the Leo woman you don't notice distinctive features as much as other signs. Her nose may be short or long, and her eyebrows are naturally high and arched. She carries a constant look of surprise and wonder, drinking in all the marvelous things in life. Her generous nature is revealed in her eyes.

Her ears are rarely displayed, since her hair usually covers them. She'll use her hair to frame her face, like a lion's mane. She may tease it into billowy folds or simply let it hang loosely. No matter how it's done, it will give her the look of a queen. She is inclined to be overly fussy about how her finely textured hair looks. If it isn't just right, it could ruin her whole day.

She has very smooth skin, which retains its velvety texture far into middle and old age. Her complexion tends to the very fair, though some incline toward the slightly ruddy. There are not many dark or olive-skinned Leo ladies. By the same token, there are not too many brunettes in her tribe. Her hair color usually ranges from pale blond to light brown.

A Leo lady is usually tall or of medium height, and her carriage is superlative! When this gal enters a room, every eye is on her. There's something truly grandiose about her, her impetuous looks, her dramatic stature, the well-timed halt when all eyes are glued to her. She possesses the faculty of causing immediate admiration and is very generous in her appreciation of compliments. When walking down the street, she does so with a queenly grace, head held high, seemingly unaware of anyone around her. She's hard to approach when walking alone, acting as if no one else exists.

She's the one who comes up with original ideas and combinations of cut and color in clothes. She prefers the extremes: cold blues and purples, hot reds and pinks; and particularly various shades of orangy reds. Her style is always first-rate and expensive. She may not always have a big budget, but what she does buy will be chic and expensive-looking. The material must be just so—she knows the difference.

No ready-made "dime-a-dozen" sweaters for Miss Leo. She has a knowledge and an insight when it comes to elegant dressing. She'll choose exquisite angoras and Scottish wools; a costly label enchants her.

She adores furs, combining a fluffy Norwegian fox stole with a tailored theater suit, or wearing a Persian lamb tunic over a brocade skirt.

If she has money, the Leo woman's wardrobe will be totally and completely elegant, right down to her underwear, which will be designed for her figure. She'll rarely ever need a girdle. Her bras are beautifully cut, and she'll buy the best hose—in all colors, to coordinate with her wardrobe.

If you spot her with a large, chunky gold chain with a dangling jewel around her neck, it's real, not costume jewelry. The desire for the extravagant really stands out in this department. She loves precious stones and can wear heavy jewelry well.

Save your pennies and spend your dollars when it comes to keeping her happy with perfume! She goes for the best—Nuit de Noël, Joy. Jasmine scents or any oil-based perfumes are preferred. She's so meticulous about bathing and cleanliness that she could be a bit annoying to someone who lives with her. She indulges herself with showers, tub baths, saunas, and massages. She takes time to rub softening creams and lotions into her skin. And she is usually overly concerned with "self."

Despite this obsession, the Leo girl really does care, and wants you to compliment and flatter her. A guy might have to be a Midas to keep her happy, but she's a treat to be around.

Where to Find Her

When trying to locate the Leo lady, you should try to find a way to be introduced to her. She is very selective about people and usually frowns on familiarity from strangers. Once introduced, however, she is very generous and very anxious to please. She loves well-timed flattery, but won't like it if you walk right up and suddenly tell her she's gorgeous.

Nine chances out of ten she will be actively involved in occupations of varying sorts, whether she needs the money or not. She has an impulsive, almost compelling desire to be the queen, the leader, always the head of the parade.

In business, there is a preference to hold an executive position, responsible only to the president or chairman of the board. When Leo is required to act, she'll readily act on her own decisions. She really doesn't like taking orders at all.

Many Leo women are doctors, surgeons, psychiatrists, or psychologists, largely because they love telling other people what to do and how to run their lives. Leos generally like to be in command of any situation. If you happen to meet such a lady when you go to find out about your sore throat or running nose, meet her equally. Accept her for her status in society. Don't overplay the male-strength angle; if you do, you won't make it. She's one way and expects you to be the same. She'll forget her friends temporarily if she's experiencing a torrid affair, and she expects you to devote your entire being to it.

If you don't, she's liable to flounce off in total anger. Anger is one thing she's never averse to expressing.

Primary Move

You've met her, you've gotten to know her best delights; now to keep her amused, provide action and movement. Take her to the horse or dog track, betting and thrilling to the excitement of it all. Or to Las Vegas, Reno, or the Bahamas for gambling. Suggest a weekend at one of these spots and she won't hesitate. She is intrigued with the jet set and the high social scene; even being a small part of it turns her on.

She's a good gambler and enjoys every aspect of challenge. Losing, she'll toss her tickets in the air in a regal fashion. If she wins, she'll run like a child and gleefully claim her winnings.

Let her know how good you are, or at least how good you think you are, but don't compete with her. She doesn't dream about castles in the sky or in the sand. Her palaces must be real. She dotes on England, manor houses, and your town's finest neighborhood.

Leo women love to dine at enchanting places, not at one of those "all-you-can-eat-for-$1.69" jobs. She dotes on glamorous, famous restaurants, the kind that make the gossip columns. She's very interested in status and position. She's not a picky eater; actually, she has a rather voluptuous appetite.

Caesar salad, hot French bread, cheese sauces, flaming duck, or shish kebab simply knock her out. She can eat a man's share of vegetables, too. You name it, she'll eat it. She likes vegetables treated with candied or sweet-and-sour sauces. Give her green beans, but with almonds and hollandaise sauce. She is turned on by spices, like dill or hot sauce. They really delight her palate. When she looks at a menu, she envisions a feast. She craves desserts with a lemon or lime flavor, and prefers anything with a combination of the tart and sweet as opposed to heavy, chocolate types of after-dinner treats.

Take her to a nightclub, but make sure a famous star is performing. She's a stickler for the proper price and place. If you take her to the theater, don't risk placing her in the balcony. She's strictly the orchestra type. She'll enjoy a drama as much as a comedy. If it's sad, she'll enjoy a terrific cry, and then put on that sparkle and smile.

She reacts too emotionally to things outside herself, with the ability to be mentally involved in other matters. But when it comes to the two of you and an inner involvement, all else really disappears.

Pre-coitus

The Leo woman is one of the most exciting love partners of all the zodiac signs. In day-to-day living she exuberantly exhibits a love of life. Her purposeful involvement in leading

The Lovers' Guide to Sensuous Astrology

others around by the ring she places in their noses is done so tactfully and lovingly, it literally becomes her second major occupation. Her first and foremost drive is one of the libido. She is clever, witty, and very independent, and is fascinated by sexual situations. In any relationship with males, she feels she's their equal. So keep in mind you're not dealing with an average woman. The true Leo woman will search out and usually find the most beautiful and expensively seductive lounging clothes and gowns available. It is here that your first clue lies.

In order to really excite and stimulate her, you must remember two very important things. First, flatter her. Flattery brings her senses to a delectable high and arouses her emotions until she feels the blood tingling close to the surface of her skin, over her entire body. She revels in your appreciation of her beauty and seductiveness. You cannot be the big, strong, silent type. Speak directly and to the point, flatter her constantly, tell her how lovely she is, how bright, how clever, how adorable, how desirable, how perfectly regal she looks. This kind of conversation will get you everywhere with a Leo woman.

Secondly, if you want to bed this lioness, give her an expensive gift such as jewelry or French candy, early in the evening. Give it to her later if it's an exciting piece of lingerie or some intricate body jewelry. Something from an antique art collection that shows excellent workmanship can enchant her. Or a new "gimmicky" cigarette lighter covered in enamel and glitter. Even if she doesn't smoke, if it's exhilarating to look at and wondrous to feel, she may carry it with her just to show it off.

The best way to please a Leo woman is to bring her a revealing negligee or an impudent nightgown trimmed in imported lace. Something that's really breathtaking and seductive. It'll be worth the investment. She won't give a second thought to popping out of what she's wearing and into that lovely new gift.

She'll walk around the room. She'll show off her body, walking gracefully, slinking like a big cat. A lioness will be graceful and very sure of herself as long as you are constantly complimentary. Admire her with your eyes as well as with verbal expressions. If you want results, this is something you must do.

The first time you make your move, be certain your apartment is the greatest, really outstanding, perfectly furnished, and accoutered with every kind of luxury, from antique lamps and tables to bearskin rugs and cashmere blankets. Unless you've got this kind of situation to offer, go to her place, not yours. There's no doubt that even the Leo woman with a moderate income will have captivatingly unique and expensive things in her home. The lioness' den is usually immaculately and elegantly put together.

The Leo lady loves your gift, and while she's prancing about, tell her she looks like an original Renoir, a shimmering jewel, a colorful butterfly, but why the restraining bra? When she hopped into your lovely gift, she left her panties on, too. This hint will do it. She'll divest herself of the flimsy panties and unsnap the restraining bra. Oh, yes, she'll cooperate. She knows why you're there; she knows why you brought the gift. This lioness isn't naïve. As long as you lead her into it and flatter her, she'll remove all encumbrances and look simply ravishing. No matter how generous nature has been to a Leo woman, her physical appearance seems to grow more succulent under the eyes of delighted male admiration.

You can express your own excitement to her very vividly. If, for example, seeing her like this has given you an erection, take her by the hand and tell her to "feel this." Leave your trousers on, unzip your fly, and guide her hand around your penis. Let her hold it as if she were clinging to a ship's mast at the height of a storm. Lean back a bit and let her pull the hard staff. By this time both hands will be "hanging on for dear life."

Her own aggressiveness comes into play quickly. Remember, she feels she's your equal. There's no man-woman thing between you. It's strictly "here are two people who want to make mad love to each other."

Coitus

Feeling very dewy between her thighs by now, she'll let go of your penis and deftly remove your trousers before you know it. Once there's clear sailing ahead, she'll be down on her knees, first savoring the tip of your penis, then avidly performing fellatio. She has a magnificent way of doing this. Somehow in her elegant manner and using no visible means of strength, she'll have you lying flat on the floor. She'll advance her second attack by holding your penis straight up in her hands, looking at it as if it were a work of art, then handling it as if she wanted the perfect feel of it for sculpturing at a later date. Then, like a hungry child, she will proceed to suck very enthusiastically.

Now she'll invite you to get into the act, probably insisting that you perform cunnilingus on her. She'll place herself, still in her precious negligee—she won't take it off—on that luxurious carpeting. The lioness will lie down beside you like a backward bookend. She'll position herself whereby she will be on her side and you will be on yours. This way, it will be easy for your mouth to reach her clitoris and for her mouth to reach your penis. The Leo woman enjoys this mutual oral lovemaking tremendously, and it can go on for a long period of time. Therefore, it's wise to gauge your tempo accordingly. Take over now; carefully and deliberately examine her with your tongue. Start just above the pubic hair, wetting it with saliva. Rub your chin gently on the matted, perfumed hairs. Work your mouth down to the lips of the vagina and tease her by darting your tongue against the lips, then toward the honeyed opening awaiting your attention. On the outside of the vagina, start above the anus with your tongue and like an ardent puppy lap up and up and up. Do this several times, and you'll turn her into a vibrantly gyrating thunderstorm. When the motion gets fast and furious, or she starts biting instead of tenderly sucking your penis, remove it from her mouth. Sit up, reach over, and face her to you. Tell her to kneel over you as you lie down. Then gently coax her hips on to your stomach, up to your chest, then on to your face. Now the tongue vigorously explores her vagina, as if reaching for the neck of the womb. She will have many orgasms and will want to assert her pleasure by reciprocating the ecstasy for you.

She will commence to experiment with her lips and tongue into all your private parts, along the cheeks of your rear end and into the nooks and crannies. If you've got dimples, she'll find them! The Leo woman's tongue is inquisitive and will ferret out all those highly sexual, sensitive places very quickly.

The Leo woman has an urgent need for many nuances in sex. She's now sitting on your lap with your penis inside her; her breasts will be practically on a par with your mouth. Nibble one nipple, then the other, as you squeeze her hips, holding her firmly on course. Caress her buttocks in fast circular spirals, pulling yourself farther and farther into her. She'll hold on to the back of the chair, using it as a rudder to steer her way through the excruciating but deliciously wonderful pain-consuming course you've set.

By the way, while some zodiac signs enjoy vulgar language during sex, never use this kind of talk with a Leo woman. She will do the most provocative unusual things and will enjoy the most sensational and unique positions in sex, but the language must always be loving, endearing, and sensual in a poetic way, using phrases of an artistic bent.

If you must vent your emotions verbally in a powerful way, just moan—it's safer.

Finale coming up! After all this action, she is ready to do it the old-fashioned way, and you're ready for your final (for that day) orgasm together.

Post-coitus

When it's over and you've both recovered your breath and senses, hopping into a shower together like two playmates is much better than remaining in bed. In fact, you've noticed, you haven't been to bed at all. That comes at another time, when you might have had a hard day at the office, or she has. A Leo woman is always busy either working in some executive position or running a charity ball.

Hop into the shower with her, and rub her briskly afterwards. Ask her to dress in something startling of her own; this will be the perfect epilogue to the perfect drama.

But beware. If you both decide to have a glass of wine and some salami on rye, very shortly it could start all over again.

The Leo woman is a very delightful individual. She enjoys intelligent conversation after sex, and very rarely wants to go right to sleep. As we have said, she would very much prefer something vigorous, a swim if it's in the afternoon, or a shower, not a bath—she's a little too prone to cleanliness to want to sit in a tub of water with a man.

Now, if you're really a glutton for sex and if you really want to turn her on for that second feature, take out the second gift you've brought for her that night. That head-whirling scent of very expensive, very French perfume. Place it in all the special places; she'll love it, and she'll be yours for as long as you want her.

VIRGO (August 22– September 22)

The Virgo Man

Recognition

Although he may be just medium tall in height, the Virgo male "walks" tall. He has an impressive way of carrying himself, giving an illusion of great height. Usually dark-complexioned, or at least boasting a healthy tan, he carries his head forward; his face is characterized by a very high forehead and large eyes that are usually clear and quiet. A full lower lip and a thick upper lip distinguish his mouth, and his hair is usually fine-textured.

If you look at him and squint your eyes, it would appear that his face is made of a series of triangles. The Virgo usually supports broad shoulders, but his arms, legs, and fingers are long and streamlined. His hands gesture beautifully, exhibiting his well-formed fingers and meticulously groomed nails. A pertinent sign to observe in the Virgo male is his walk. He moves briskly, but often with a slight hitch in his stride, as he bears more pressure on one foot than on the other. It's one of those odd occurrences with this sign of the zodiac, and difficult to explain. Nevertheless, this unusual movement is no impediment to his speed.

On the other hand, many Virgoans are blessed with long life, and happily for them, carry a youthful appearance into late middle age. It's simple to single him out in a crowd, because even at a party he'll most likely be standing center stage with a questioning gaze, observing others, listening to their conversations, and deciding who's just the right one to talk to!

He's almost always carefully groomed, with fingernails buffed and shiny. Generally, all facial hair is removed, and you seldom if ever see a Virgo with a moustache or beard. His hair, although fine, will be styled to disguise its true texture, covering his pate in an attractive manner. But he's somewhat of a hypochondriac, this Virgo. It's not that he has chronic bad health, but he believes in that old adage "An ounce of prevention is worth a pound of cure," and his medicine cabinet is likely bulging with preventive cures.

The Virgo man is economical, spending only when he realizes every penny's worth. He's fastidious when it comes to romance, is horrified by vulgarity, and is disenchanted with anyone who is careless in grooming or sloppy in dress. This attitude is something to keep in mind when you're ready to make your move. You should religiously attend to those beauty chores like plucking your eyebrows, doing your nails, and washing your hair, because you never know which day Virgo will be filling an important place in your life.

Time is of the essence for him, and he feels it a personal affront if he's kept waiting, and likewise is adamant about being punctual himself.

An aspect of his makeup that he must watch is overt criticism of others, all the while abhorring criticism of himself. It's a troubling part of his nature to be impatient with less than perfection, and he just can't see the probability or possibility that he could be wrong. However, he's bright and could learn early in life to keep his more caustic and biting comments to himself.

His clothing is spic and span, utilizing simple colors like blacks, grays, and whites, with a touch of blue as an accessory in sport and business clothes. This man is neat to the point of perfection. If he lives in the north, he'll wear vests, and where hats are stylish, he'll wear one, no matter the temperature. He'll fold his gloves carefully and place them tidily in his pocket or briefcase. His methodical sense of precision carries over into his working habits, and if he leaves for work at 8:00 A.M., has lunch at 12:30, gets home at exactly 6:15, rests for an hour and a half, spends an hour at dinner, and winds up reading or watching TV until 11:30, you can be sure he'll repeat the routine five days a week. Succinct and concise, that's the Virgo man.

The Virgo man is health-food-oriented, high on decaffeinated coffee, wheat germ, and soybeans, and knows the content of most cans on the supermarket shelf, along with the additives therein. He knows the vitamin value of each type of meat, fish, or fowl, and which part of his body it serves. Many Virgoans are vegetarians, going for big salads, honey instead of sugar, and nonfat or buttermilk as opposed to the homogenized variety.

Soda pop is veritable poison to the Virgo, and potato chips are mankind's destruction. He'll snack on celery and cheese with rye crackers, or bran muffins, oat cakes, and rice patties. Gelatin of any flavor suits him, because it's protein-high and nonfattening. When you feed him, make sure the dishes are shiny, the silverware free of any water spots or grease, and the crystal minus lipstick marks.

Where to Find Him

The naturally predominant factor in "running down" the Virgo male is giving great thought to his correct and proper attitudes to all kinds of work, pleasure, or avocations.

Demands, made by himself on himself, preclude any disposition toward the free-and-easy occupation or the casually relaxed endeavor.

He cries for and gets those duties that are almost always exhausting to others, enormously boring to most—but to him the main reason for living. Everything in its place, properly done.

He's likely to be found in large numbers in clinics or hospitals, where his talent for x-ray, radiology, nutrition, and pharmacy will be of great value. Virgo tends toward the art of medicine. His understanding of the intricacies of the delicate machinery of the human body and an inborn precise nature mark him as the surgeon. Otherwise, his pursuits are largely intellectual, with an avid interest in life's important things, like government work in the ecological fields. Another possibility is zoology, working with chromosomes and interbreeding, perhaps a study of how wild animals survive and propagate in captivity.

Virgo can be a fluent negotiator who can handle deals for others better than for himself. The demand for careful work in making fine furniture or cabinetry is quite often an area of occupation that calls the Virgo.

Although he enjoys a good laugh, the basis of it is usually contained in a play on words or some nonsensical remark by an "egghead" that would pass over the heads of most who heard it. He does have a sense of humor, more the wry or pun-making sort. Slapstick leaves him cold.

He's very unpretentious in his living habits, affecting a spartan existence. Self-discipline can be rewarding, and in his case those extra coupons he clips from his gold bonds are due to his programs of self-imposed savings.

That early-morning work-out on his bedroom floor, counting up to fifty for each of the ten exercises he does day in and day out, pays off in a fine, tight body like that of a much younger man.

His sexual habits are regular, demanding, and healthy, just like everything else about him. One must eat, drink, exercise, sleep, and . . . have sex to be mentally and physically well.

Any entertainment he seeks is likely to verge on the intellectual—lectures, courses in Oriental cultures, the newest foods to prolong the good life, always the unusual and decidedly mental and provocative for the Virgo male.

He enjoys fishing because it's a simple occupation and the results are edible. Planting a vegetable garden and tending to it appeals to his methodical soul. He'll water, weed, and spade it with constancy, apply the proper chemicals in the ground, and spray it for insects.

Canoeing is a nice, easy way to pass the time and gives him a moment's pause from his rather headlong intellectual pursuits. Winter sports could include either cheering for his favorite hockey team or doing precision figure eights on the ice himself.

He skis, not just for fun, but for the proper body discipline of moving, walking, jumping, and even tumbling down—then, too, there's all that great oxygen to fill his healthy lungs.

If you've never known the immense pleasure of constant good health and a true feeling of well-being, then find the Virgo man, follow his lead, and learn to live again.

Primary Move

Just offhandedly "giving it a whirl" to meet the Virgo would be a big mistake. He's such a pedantic kind of guy, somewhat set in his ways, that careful thought and a lot of preparation should precede your first invitation to the Virgo male. Since you know he's into health foods and that physical people are those he admires, invite him to a social gathering in your home. Try to invite a few guests who share his interests, and serve raw vegetables and nuts and anything else that looks appealing on the shelves of the local health-food store. It will definitely turn on the Virgo man. In fact, you could become so interested, you might even turn into a health addict yourself, up to your eyeballs in vitamin C and rose hips. Choose something white or light blue to wear. He loves those colors, and make certain your nail polish isn't chipped, your hair is brushed to gleaming, and your makeup carefully and subtly applied. He won't object to a neat pants suit but will prefer you in a dress; make a note to pull your panty hose tight. Stockings sagging on the ankles or wrinkling at the knee is the height of sloppiness to Virgo.

After the rest of your guests go home, take him out on the balcony and later serve him a cup of decaffeinated coffee. After coffee, suggest showing him the saunas in the building's health club, and if you're aggressive enough (and better be, this is your moment), hint at taking one with him. Once again his habit patterns will "hop to"; and while you're cozily perspiring together, towel-wrapped, in the hot sauna, his fading inhibitions should melt away. See to it that they do.

Pre-coitus

Virgo seems totally unaware of his own sensuality, yet he's extremely passionate. His carefully controlled outward appearance masks his inner passion and tends to impart a cool image. Don't let this facade fool you. He wants the proper someone to break through, but you've got to do it right.

Valiantly the Virgo man will stick to his known principles of spartan living. He can't compute the myriad subtleties of life, in sex particularly, and see why they're so desirable to some. In other words, all fun and games are played by the book. Deviations must be thought out carefully, but if you have a good imagination, you can conceive a very antiseptic sexual adventure with him simply by employing his needs to your best advantage.

Cleanliness and a pattern that doesn't change abruptly are the keynote. After sauna, the body is in a wondrous state of relaxation, purged of all impurities. Why not a nice soapy shower together? Soap, the bane of existence to small boys, is the happiness of life to the Virgo man.

"O.K., coach, to the showers!" Let him regulate the faucets. It won't be his fingers, but icy fingers of water down your spine. He dotes on spartan ways, as you know, and a brisk, cold shower is the "thing." Try the temperature with your hand; if it's too cold, hop around from one foot to the other, laughingly complaining that the frigid cold makes a frigid you. Virgo is a tall and hard-boned fellow, trim and well-cared-for, a treat for your eyes. He may not understand your "carrying on", but martyrlike, he'll turn the hot-water spigot. Now the shower becomes as delicious as a warm spring rain.

"Let's go! It's great, once you duck!" Since you'll be exhilarating sexually in the water, prepare the field of play by placing thick towels on the bottom of the tub. You don't want any inadvertent accidents. Climb in together, like two water sprites.

Let him be closest to the shower spray. Soap up a washcloth with pleasant-smelling creamy soap.

Now, starting with his back, scrub his shoulders, down his arms, under his arms, down the small of his back, between his cheeks.

Just for fun, while the cloth is working its way down Virgo's long thigh, let your other hand wash his penis and testicles. Undoubtedly your efforts will be rewarded by an immediate hard-on.

Don't bother washing the toes; let them go. After all, why miss an opportunity like this? By gently pulling on his penis, turn him around. Meanwhile, in the kneeling position you now assume, the rushing water is playing over your hair, face, and in your eyes and ears. But it's not as loud as the beating in your breast. Take his penis in both hands and place the tip of his pendulum in your mouth. There's no soapy taste, just a great heat emanating from the head, magnified in its intensity by the comparison of spring rain turned to frosty hail pounding on your back. Place your tongue in the Virgo's urethra, jabbing it between the opening with surgical preciseness. Move closer now, putting your face against his wet and curly pubic hair. Squirm sideways and position yourself to encase the base of his penis in your mouth, stroking its length with your hand.

Since cleanliness is the order of the moment, crawl over to the edge of the tub, flick the cap off the toothpaste tube you previously placed there for easy access. While clinging to his penis for support, squeeze a good supply of the pepperminty cream in your mouth. The tingling frosty sensation caused by the toothpaste combined with your own efforts will bring him to the peak of sensation.

The Lovers' Guide to Sensuous Astrology   89

Not a vestige of warm water is left, and the shower is arctic cold as his own vital shower explodes in your mouth, sexy-hot. Yes, you'd like more, but don't push your luck. Turn off the faucets and let him dry your body thoroughly with a towel. He may not be too inventive, but his educated hands can give you the release you need as his long forefinger meets the inside of your vagina. While he's holding you in one arm, with his other hand within, rub his back with the towel. Stand on tippy-toe, stretching your body up and down as you reach behind him to dry his lean figure. Your body action, simultaneous with his keen fingering, should do it. That's g-o-o-d!

His and her hair's wet. Your electric hand hair dryer is adaptable, cool or warm air. Ask him to turn it to warm and pass the dryer over and around your head. Hair dry now, why stop there? Try a warm air flow on your damp pubic hair. Your clitoris, sensitive to his touch and the warm temperature, will extend itself, begging for more attention. Soothingly, he can stroke you, bringing forth a delightful clitoral orgasm.

Coitus

Fraternizing with your Virgoan male has been more water polo than romance. Hair and body dried now and primed for more, your Virgo man is ready to try for a mutual orgasm. On to the boudoir, both of you shiny clean from top to toe, ready for further pleasures in bed this time. But first, stop in front of the full-length mirror in your bedroom, admiring yourselves as you stand side-by-side. Then touch him while watching yourself doing this. Ask him to fondle your breasts. Just moving your respective hands jointly is thrilling stimulation on a multiple sensory plane. He has to react again from sexuality itself, watching the reflection as you manipulate each other's bodies. It's most alluring.

Now that you're feeling dizzy from the energizing bathroom calisthenics and mirror tricks, a quiet coitus in a soundless, uncluttered room is the denouement of the evening. The Virgo male will put away his mental score cards, rules, and regulations as he surrenders to encirclement by your arms, your legs, and finally your nest of love.

Post-coitus

Pink and pearly-gray bands of color dress the early-morning sky, as the day comes into being.

The night and its trenchant activity past, you sleep for hours, engrossed in your dreams, snugly wrapped in sweet-smelling blankets, feathery pillows, and his staunch maleness.

Congratulations. You now have a roommate of simple needs and sterile (?) habits for as long as you like.

The Virgo Woman

Recognition

Very much like the Leo woman in her tendency to appear regal, although she's rarely very tall, the Virgo woman is slim, trim, and carries herself extremely well. Her face is usually oval, with a high forehead and eyes very far apart. Those eyes have a direct gaze, for this lady is a seeker of truth, dealing in realities, somehow unable to function as well in subtleties or surreptitious matters or remarks. She says it as it is; there's no coquetry about her at all.

Her hair is usually dark and fine. The nose is straight and of medium size, not often commanding too much attention one way or the other. Her long legs seem like two young willow trees, supple and flexible. If she's into exercising or dancing for figure control (and she probably is), you'll find the calf muscle beautifully developed. Although many Virgo girls have large feet, they don't really seem quite that large. The size seems fit to carry her tall, well-proportioned, tight-muscled body. Her upper lip is full, and her expression is determined and thoughtful. You'll almost never hear her ripping someone up the back out of their presence or indulging in babbling unkind gossip.

Fortunately for her, she tans like a dream, and her usually olive complexion doesn't wrinkle easily from all that sun. She's blessed with the look of a perennial sophomore all through life.

You can spot the Virgo gal by her walk—brisk, meaningful, and determined. She has a way of always looking well-groomed, meticulous, and manicured, her eyebrows beautifully arched and her coiffure stressing every hair in place. Her striving for perfection can be a frustrating problem for the Virgo woman, because, being human, neither she nor anyone else could ever make the grade. Yet, just accepting this fact is an impossibility to her. She'll continue to reach for the incredible mark of perfection.

Her personality is one of a critical nature, interesting and intellectual always, finding life difficult if she has to handle anything devious or false. She has an obvious need for a partner, one who loves totally. Conversely, she's not the jealous sort, and neither is she overly possessive, but she demands fidelity and a deep, meaningful love in her relationships. She's not one for many short-lived, in-and-out affairs.

If the Virgo woman doesn't really "feel," it's difficult for her to maintain an intimate involvement. But when the right man appears, it's total immersion for her.

She's prompt always, possibly more so than any other sign. She despises bad language and is genuinely shocked when uncouth words or phrases are tossed around. She simply can't handle it.

It's her thinking that, even if we're way past the Victorian era, there's no reason why a man cannot be a perfect gentleman. She likes to have doors opened for her, her coat removed. She likes to be helped with her bundles, and appreciates it if you hail a cab. These are musts with the Virgo lady. She's feminine in the extreme, yet totally independent, almost never a flirt, and wouldn't think of batting her eyelashes or wiggling her fanny. And she'd rather do without physical intimacy than be involved in an affair that's not good for her.

She has an excellent memory, and in business or in private life will hold a secret to the death. She's trustworthy and doesn't talk about private matters, yours or hers. Although not a fighter, she'll set up opposition and be overly critical in some matters. That's her big problem—she expects perfection from others, at least enough "try" expended to fulfill their own potential, no matter how limited it might be. She'll approach a difficult subject quietly, practically, and subtly, a tact likely to drive the object of all this right out of his skin.

Virgo women are not highly emotional unless they're deeply in love. Most feel they are born to please, serve, and instruct, utterly charming in all phases of their being.

In the matter of clothes, she prefers basic colors, like navy blues, blacks, grays, and varying shades of those hues. Comfort and good looks are her goals in this field, with a fine sense of accessory coordination. In an area where hats are worn, she'll be wearing a chic and stylish one. Looking sloppy only when she is depressed, and that's rare, her disregard of her appearance is usually a result of loneliness. Her high ideals and values make it hard for her to find the proper partner. Jewelry is not terribly important to the Virgo female, unless it's in the accessory line, and it should be real or of the very expensive costume variety.

If you want to diet, choose the Virgo woman as a dining partner. She'll be delighted to go along with you, a health-food and proper-diet addict to the core. In fact, it's one of the few areas in which she's truly vehement, even "way-out." She enjoys preparing food and making it attractive, but since food to her is primarily for energy, salads rate high on her chart, with all members of the lettuce family, including dandelion greens, raw carrots, onions—anything that's good and healthy. She likes cheeses, but natural ones, not pasteurized or manufactured, and she eschews the overly odorous types. Unsalted, oilless roasted nuts, yogurt, turnips, squash—all the kinds of vegetables children learn to hate—simple desserts or none, but if she does indulge, it will definitely not be fattening.

Virgo's cologne will be fresh, light, and cleanly scented. She'll use soaps that are good for her skin, and rub her body with oils to keep the texture soft. The body and the mind are important to this lady, and never too much time can be spent on improving both. Only when emotionally disturbed does she neglect important matters, and she'll fight herself to stay "up," despising herself or anyone else who wallows in "the blues."

Where to Find Her

Her interest in food from a nutritional standpoint rather than as a chef will often draw the Virgo woman to food production and service on a large scale, such as in universities or health centers, or even supermarkets. She's a logical reasoner, dedicated to serving a purpose or the demands of others, and you may find her in charitable institutions, never as a volunteer but on a paid basis as an administrator or organizing committees to get work done. She understands money and handles it well, but has no particular desire to be wealthy. Money is for well-being, period!

She'd make a fine dietician or hygienist and could succeed as a doctor, dentist, nurse, lab technician, or geologist because she enjoys doing important, detailed assignments and work that benefits others. A Virgo woman makes an excellent secretary, and if she has a sympathetic boss who'll give her the go-ahead, she'll follow through and be intensely loyal as well as extremely defensive where people she respects are concerned. A personnel agency would be a great place to locate her, because she'd be helping others find their proper niche.

Some of our finest writers are Virgoans, particularly in the vein of "how-to" books, and because they are critical souls, make fine observers of the theatrical scene in newspapers or write columns on the editorial page. And no matter whether you still call them efficiency experts or the newer label, management consultants, Virgo women are tops in this field.

As for sports, there is interest, but Virgos are not buffs. Football, baseball, basketball, and tennis can be interesting, but not essential. What she does like is yoga, isometrics, any gymnastic activity. She really enjoys skiing because of the great outdoors, the purity, cleanliness, and virtue of all that snow, which renews her spirit and makes her feel whole again if she's been low.

Primary Move

The primary approach to the Virgo female is somewhat different from that of other signs. Unless you're really sure of her, the best move is the accidental meeting or an introduction through a mutual friend. You might meet her in a class, in the library studying, or taking a course in adult education, most likely psychology. If you dress casually, be sure you're clean and attractive, never too colorful or showy. Be well-manicured, closely shaved, with a light, spicy cologne, and you hair well-groomed. You have really got to look like a walking mannequin to this lady. Give her the idea you're striving for perfection, just as she does.

You can chat with her about many things, how puzzling other people are, the world situation, etc., and give her an opportunity to show you what a logical thinker she is. Play the critic with her and you'll regret it. Remember, she's a super critic herself, so be nice, affable, and interested. Always the perfect gentleman. Open the classroom door for her, invite her for a glass of milk, never coffee—that's not healthy. Hold out her chair, help her with her sweater or coat, because the niceties are meaningful to her. After some talk and refreshment for this night, it's time to go home. Don't press for fun and games too soon with a Virgo. Walk her to her car, ask her for the keys, open the door, and when she's inside, lock it. As an afterthought (seemingly) knock on the window and ask if she'd like to join you in a yoga session. She knows you're a student, although you discussed it only offhandedly. Tell her that you have a striking meditation room she'd enjoy seeing. She'll accept. If it's for Saturday night at eight P.M., the Virgo gal will ring your doorbell right on the dot.

Pre-coitus

It must be her down-to-earth, modest, hard-working nature and wholesome attractiveness that grab you. Certainly, of all the signs of the zodiac, the Virgo woman is probably the least addictive to sex. Her need is one involved in total health. One must eat properly, get enough sleep, and take the right amount of exercise; sexually speaking, when the physical need intrudes on the day-to-day activities, for health's sake, one must!

There's no doubt her earnestness, brisk step, healthy skin, and radiant smile of well-being are attractive. A wholesome morsel, explicit and detailed in her approach to sex. A healthy body makes a clear and sensitive mind. Yes, that's it. She's like a sunflower turning her head to the sun, or a rainbow at the end of a storm.

Whether you're physically oriented to hard exercise or not, it's sylish these days to participate in yoga, with its varied gentle stretching and deep-breathing exercises that help keep you fit. The Virgo woman is generally endowed with excellent good looks throughout life. Her youthful attitudes and posture maintenance indicate she's dabbled in the art of yoga herself. Suffice to say, whether it's so or not, a little yoga meditation and positioning could encourage physical contact and who knows what else?

While chatting with her, you have convinced her that

you're a master in the art of food intake, body care, and spiritual advancement.

It's advisable that you spend more than a mere few days developing your yoga positions and breathing techniques. To utilize this decoy properly, you must be adept at it.

Since the dining room is the easiest from which you can remove furniture, it is here that you'll assemble a room dedicated to mind-and-body discipline. Glamorize it with Indian print tablecloths making do as drapes, and your buffet an altar of many sweet-smelling candles. Incense burning in two or three places adds just that perfect Eastern touch.

No electric lights, just the mystic sight of the Far East, with the stereo playing quietly some unique music. There is the sound of bells tinkling and pipes plaintively wailing as she enters your room of meditation at eight P.M. sharp. Even a stage director and designer couldn't have achieved a better effect.

The dress for this transcendental meeting is leotards for her and a tight bathing suit for you. A woman of the most moderate sexual impulses finds her thighs begin to sizzle when she sees your masculine figure in a form-fitting loincloth, genitals enclosed but bulging their presence, buttocks exposed, with the rear of the suit cutting a swath between your cheeks.

With most serious intent, lead her to the mystic mark indicated by a crystal ball. Seat her on the floor on one side of the ball, you opposite her.

Explain that first one must clear the mind of all extraneous thought, and that concentrating on the crystal ball will help accomplish this purpose.

You seat yourself in the half-lotus position by placing your right foot against the inside of your upper-left thigh.

With agility place your left foot in the cleft of your right leg. Sitting there like a young Buddha with your crotch sending Morse code across the crystal ball, she can hardly clear her mind, much less concentrate. You're not at all surprised to see her assume the half-lotus more swiftly and with greater precision than you. Oh, your hunch was right. There'll be no pulled muscles tonight; she knows her stuff.

Sitting there lotuslike, your bikini is uncomfortably confining and is crawling up farther and farther, making your concentration more improbable. As you start to squirm, Virgo suggests that if you remove your bathing suit, you'd be more comfortable, and assures you at the same time that it would be no embarrassment to her at all. A body is a body is a body! In fact, she'll remove her leotard so you'll know she understands. There you are, the crystal ball reflecting the red candlelight turning your penis a pinkish healthy hue.

Somehow this mystical meditation sends telepathic messages to his lowness, as he shortly becomes his highness. She can't help but notice your state of excitement. While she's still in her lotus position, you'll have no problem at all making an introduction.

Coitus

You hold your penis in both hands, moving from your half-lotus into proper body position for a knee-and-thigh stretch. The soles of your feet together, gently bring them closer to your body, knees flat on the floor. As you're rotating your penis by the neck, beckon her to join you in a knee-and-thigh stretch on your lap, then extend your legs to a Y position. There's just no place to put your penis once your Virgo's set but to tuck him in between her limber thighs and rotate an inch of it into the mouth of her vagina. The sensation is miraculous, and her ability to clear her mind is instantaneous. No thoughts, just a cosmic oneness with all of mankind, but particularly with you under the circumstances.

Makes no difference if she cons herself into this intercourse for health jazz. If it's a rationale permitting your enjoyment of your Virgo woman, let be what may be. Meanwhile, back at the vortex, the waters are running deep and your penis is now caught up in the action of her whirlpool. Round and round she moves, and then counterclockwise. She shifts and shoves, then round and round again. A maelstrom of pleasure.

She likes the way you practice your yoga exercises, and really with the spirit of things now, she suggests the cobra. She becomes the serpent, lying on her abdomen flat on the floor. Making a few minor adjustments to the cobra yoga, she spreads her legs and asks you to meet her again on that high plateau of exquisite sensitivity. You're ready to oblige and satisfy your Virgo girl. Her wholesomeness is surpassed only by her limber and giving body. You place your abdomen against her back, but in a kneeling position. Her legs are spread for your convenience. So, go! This time the action is so fast and furious that you and three of the five candles blow out simultaneously.

Karma paid, she asks for the route to the nearest rest room. You follow, suggesting a brisk shower together. Somehow, your East Indian intuition tells you to do just that, shower, no yoga hanky-panky.

Fresh and pink and smelling like soap, you both enjoy the playful maneuver of rubbing each other dry with a Turkish towel.

Part of her sterling character is represented by her thoughtfulness of others. Afraid you may be tired after the recent sexual interlude, she insists that you have a good massage, then a good sleep.

Post-coitus

You would think that a healthy buck like you would cater to the little Virgo gal after such a meaningful meditation session. Not this miss. She's ready to see that all's well with your body as well as your spirit.

Using a handy bottle of hand cream, she starts a finger and heel of the hand massage, not to stimulate, but to relax the body. She begins at your feet, and you're fast asleep before she reaches the lumbar region of your back. She is really something else. A perfect partner. Healthy, strong, sensitive to soul, and a great masseuse. It's understandable now, your intense desire for this Virgo woman.

LIBRA (September 23–October 22)

The Libra Man

Recognition

He's a great-looking guy, the Libran, supremely well put together. Not overly handsome, but tremendously attractive. His face is usually round or oval, with a definite chin enhanced by a dimple. He's not necessarily rugged-looking, but very masculine.

The Libran's skull is round, beautifully shaped, with hair ranging from sandy blond to light brunette. Oh, his eyes! The Libran more often than not has a veritable monopoly on the brightest, most heavenly blues, from aquamarine to sky blue, going into soft grays. What's more, these smiling eyes have a liquid look even when they're an occasional dreamy brown. Perfectly shaped eyebrows frame those marvelous eyes.

The features are neither large nor small, but very regular and well-placed. A Grecian-looking nose, long and attractive, with nicely flared nostrils. Not always perfect, but very good-looking. His ears are usually close against his head.

The Libra male has a quiet dynamism about him. Even when he needs a shave, there's an undeniable elegance about his looks.

When you speak of manly grace, look to the Libran. Usually slender and erect, his physique is beautifully refined and elegant. His arms are long and firm, with well-shaped fingers and fingernails, more than likely manicured.

The Libran strides gracefully, and though he's often a little thin in the thigh and knee area, he carries himself so wonderfully that these small defects are practically invisible.

They're a strange group, these Librans, obviously lovers of mankind, friendly, and helpful; yet when you get too close, too intimate, they will want to make a switch. It's not that they're bored, but in their own minds they want to spread the goodness around.

He enjoys dressing well in a simple sport shirt and elegant slacks. After a brisk shower, a fine cologne, and into elegant clothes, he's ready for anything, because he's being himself.

Colors related to nature are what excite the Libra male. He goes for quiet shades of cocoa, beige, ecru, or white, with pin checks and very small plaids. Although he tends toward monotones in dress, he'll swing to pale or light sapphire blues for contrast. It's fine quality of product and excellent materials that fascinate a Libran. While he rarely wears brilliant shades, the more flamboyant colors of nature—green, yellow, pink, and purple—have great eye appeal for him.

As far as jewelry goes, he might wear a school ring (because he more than likely went to a good school) or a fraternity pin, but he dislikes fakery, wearing only the real thing.

In the choice of food, the Libran's basic honesty and love of nature prevail. If it's caviar, it's got to be black and salty. If it's asparagus, he wants it fresh and green, with no fancy sauces. Because of his preference for the natural qualities of life, women and food must have the ring of truth. While dining, he prefers simple, neat surroundings with the proper amount of silverware for all courses and a table set to please the eye. He doesn't tend to overeat, and keeps away from synthetics or preservatives used in food. He's not the guy you'll stop with to have a hot dog or hamburger.

Eggs or soufflés appeal to him, along with dry wines. The taste of mint really excites him, as does the tartness of raspberry or anything that produces a mouth-watering savory sensation, a factor which could contribute to his sensuous nature.

Where to Find Him

This man loves to laugh and has an inner gaiety about him that's most appealing. He chuckles a great deal, rarely guffaws, and has a variety of little intimate smiles for you. The

Libran male has a positive yearning for old-time classical comedy movies, with Chaplin, Ben Turpin, and Ben Blue.

Golf's all right, but more because it gets him outside in a beautiful natural environment than the desire to be a champion. He likes bridge, too, because it's a clean-cut game with no subtle rules; everything about it is specific. The Libran finds it hard to make decisions, and as an alternative, ruthlessly researches a problem. This gentleman goes by the book.

You'll find lots of Librans performing in the theater. They make splendid actors, having the ability to inject feeling into a role and to perform convincingly, unless the part is one of a violent nature. As a producer, he has a winning way of raising money. He will lay his cards on the table. Because he can't come up with swift, adroit decisions, he makes a poor lawyer. But when there are basic concepts to consider, like building an edifice or designing an office, the Libran will excel as architect or decorator.

You might find him in the presumably boring confines of an insurance company, toiling as a statistician. Dealing with facts all day wouldn't bother him one bit. He's discreet, conservative, and steadfast in his thinking, yet he's an extremely amorous individual.

Primary Move

The Libran is honest, a "say-it-like-it-is" guy. You can suggest the simplest pleasures, like ice-skating, to him, and he'll respond. Hold hands while you skate, because this man is very attuned to any kind of pass, but be honest and not overly aggressive about it. Tell him how good-looking he is, because he positively dotes on flattery, although it's not absolutely necessary to his personal happiness.

Disagree with him and you might be headed for trouble. He's not totally opinionated, but being argumentative will shake him up, and this guy shouldn't be shook!

The best shot is to invite him to your home for bridge at eight P.M. Ask two dear friends to join you, but make sure they play like "Hoyle." The Libran likes to be mentally stimulated, so between rubbers inject subjects like current developments in medicine or business, but keep off the violent stuff. He is concerned about your being interested in reality and today.

When you dress for him, wear what looks best on you, but

most often you can't go wrong with shades of blue, for that color most attracts him.

Pre-coitus

You've played the cards well and found yourself the dummy half the time. He played the hands to perfection. As partners, you two make a great team. Some smart dummy!

Your Libran having won each rubber with amazing facility, you're assured of a happy man. He needs no reassurance, no scales to weigh the facts. The winning score card in black and white states the case.

Folding up the card table after friends have gone, rinsing glasses, and cleaning out ashtrays is the preliminary. These homey acts allow him the time to decide what you've got in mind. As mentioned, he never misses a pass. Just a nudge or two in the right direction, and he'll take it from there.

No "Should we, shouldn't we" on your part. A definite "Yes! We will!" as you graciously extend your hands to him in thanks for all his help.

This gorgeous hunk of man will undoubtedly react as the male gender always does and be quite accommodating. Bend his head to yours, be frank that you're aching for a kiss to show your gratitude. Even though he's so attractively masculine, don't expect him to be a ruthless lover.

He's slow and sure and particularly affectionate. Smooth and endearing. The most violent he becomes is to nibble on your ear. Then he'll kiss you lightly along your cheek to your lips. Holding you closer, he'll impart a delicious sigh of surrender, as he firmly kisses you. His kisses are long and wondrous, stirring and insistent, precious and prodding—a combination of all your dreams come to life.

After what seems a velvety, black eternity of soft and luscious lips, he'll pull away and start again, this time kissing with his mouth open, then tremulously slipping his tongue along the ridge of your front teeth. On he goes, seeking the soft pads of your inner cheek, embracing you tighter and tighter with each exploration.

He's deliberate as he motions for you to remove your clothes. As if hypnotized by his manly good looks, you automatically shift easily out of backless pumps and a simple lounging robe.

Like a law clerk, thumbing each legal page with concentration, he's unbuttoning his shirt, relishing the delay of contact.

He reveals his well-proportioned chest and slim hips—he is a delicious study of manhood.

Pre-planning and thinking ahead on your part make for success with the Libra male. Walking into your foyer, you remove your fur spread from your hall storage closet, placing it elegantly on the floor along with two downy pillows encased in sapphire blue satin. The usually unexcited Libran is enchanted by your suggestion, and lies down, his full six feet creating a picture sensational enough for the center fold of *Cosmopolitan* magazine.

Drink him in with your eyes, then suck him up with your mouth. Fellatio, expertly attended to, will thrill your glamorous guy. Luxuriating on soft mink, he looks like a potentate, rolling his head in utter delirium on the satin pillows. The Libran male's sensuous nature seems fulfilled by your understanding of the finer things in life. If he appears to be asleep, don't be fooled. He loves your approach, and really being himself is complimentary to you. He prefers you continue rather than make a decision as to what to initiate himself.

You seem to know the innermost sentiments of sexual refinement for his taste. Although he's not a sybarite, he's glorying in all this attention. His virile body retains its extended penis, standing up in royal command. A silent order, given by the sheik's scepter, demands action. Lie down and ask the princely Libran to place his knees under your arms, steering his penis to a position so you can leisurely enjoy rolling it around in your mouth.

Coitus

Amazingly so, the Libran's control is fantastic. Somehow, mind over matter results in his enormous metallike erection, retaining its full length and strength long after most others would have withered.

Your truth-seeker is primed to continue. He flicks off the lights and ignites the incense candles in your foyer sconces. The room is now luminously radiant. His splendid body lit by candleglow, your own requirements reach a point of spontaneous combustion.

As you look at his graceful body lying on his side facing you, the spark from his cigarette glimmering about the fine features of his face, your patience is at an end. Aware of your momentous need, with no reluctance he extinguishes the fiery tip. As he bends across you to reach the ashtray, adroitly guide his personal fiery tip to your eager vagina. Side-by-side in a new and harmonious feeling. As you move together in a steady rhythm, the fur, pillows, floor, room, and building disappear. You are entwined on a magic carpet, carried away to exotic places, never to return to this dimension. The tempo increases rapidly. Between the friction from the silky rug and the even more titillating sensations, your grinding movements are causing you both to experience explosive orgasm. The ride on the magic carpet is over for the moment.

Post-coitus

Snug as two bugs in the rug, you cover him with a part of the mink throw, seeing that it embraces his broad chest and slender hips.

A lovely sight as he sleeps, and you're the ever-watchful protector. Memories of the past hour keep you awake, but wakefulness just renews your sureness that Libra man is for you.

Another hour passes, and he stirs. "How about a sandwich?"

A sandwich? He's back on earth, concerned about his appetite, and you're off somewhere reliving those precious moments.

"How about roast beef with horseradish dressing?" Oh, that's great, says he, and his long form rises from the floor, headed for the john and a shower.

Prepare his bed, watch over his food, and give him what he wants when he so graciously wants it, and trip number two on your magic carpet comes again soon.

The Libra Woman

Recognition

Little Bo-Peep must have been a Libra woman, because she has the charming little oval face that one identifies with the diminutive shepherdess. Her features are in balance, just as the sign itself represents balance. Libra lady has beautiful skin, really exquisite, and not prone to eruptions, marks or blemishes. Conversely, she has to work hard to keep her skin clean, and uses little makeup because of her sensitivity to cosmetics. Good grooming habits peculiar to the Libra female are one of the things responsible for keeping her face unlined into late middle age and beyond.

Her hair is either lightly curling, with little tendrils on her forehead, or it's straight and smooth. The texture is rarely bushy, but has a soft silky touch, very easy to manage. The color ranges from brown to black, and you won't often find a blond in this tribe, unless she "does it herself."

She's well put together, Ms. Libra, but her personal tidiness doesn't carry over into her housekeeping. Usually she's somewhat careless in that area.

Her mouth sometimes looks like a Kewpie doll's, with a full upper lip, small and pouting; her lower lip is small but full, as if bee-stung. Perennially she looks as if waiting to be kissed or in the process of throwing a kiss your way. The cheeks are more than likely dimpled—one on each side.

The Libra woman's nose is average, nothing outstanding, but not hard to deal with either. She has a natural fresh, comely look, being well-proportioned and very slender during her youth. Her key word is not "chic," but "neat," smartly dressed always.

Latest U.S. Government tests of all cigarettes show True is lower in both tar and nicotine than 98% of all other cigarettes sold.

Think about it.
Shouldn't your next cigarette be True?

Regular: 11 mg. "tar", 0.7 mg. nicotine,
Menthol: 12 mg. "tar", 0.7 mg. nicotine, av. per cigarette, FTC Report Mar. '74.

Latest U.S. Government tests of all menthol cigarettes show True is lower in both tar and nicotine than 98% of all other menthols sold.

Think about it.
Shouldn't your next cigarette be True?

Warning: The Surgeon General Has Determined That Cigarette Smoking Is Dangerous to Your Health.

© Lorillard 1974

Even though her features suggest a tiny girl, Lady Libra is usually of middle height, or tall and slender. Many Librans are fashion models.

They're natural-born flirts, these gals, the eyes delivering an unmistakable message of "come hither." But then the hand goes up, meaning "stay away." They really don't know what they want, these fascinating creatures; their very imbalance in deciding what's best is offset by their total balance in their great figures and in their way of life. They strive for schedule and good performance.

Librans avoid extreme fads when it comes to clothes. Their balance again combines with an innate knowledge of style, what looks good *on* them and *to* them. The little basic black dress, for instance, with pearls, of course, is *de rigueur*. They generally won't go for lacy see-through, or shed their bras for fashion effect. They know they're exciting and wholesomely sexy without all that exposure, and prefer well-cut satins or velvets in dark crimson, ruby, or port. Or wine-colored suits in flannel, equipped with smart gray accessories. Deep-toned colors appeal to these girls, and a particular favorite is sapphire blue. Along with ruby reds and blacks, sapphire and sister blues reflect her desire to seem reserved and stunning at the same time.

Jewelry is very much on the conservative side with these ladies. They'll affect beautiful gold pieces, maybe chunky, but only of the finest design, as well as diamonds or star sapphires. Stones of a semiprecious nature are desirable as long as they're blue. She likes pearls, too, because they're decorous, like the image she tries to create. Her delight in wristwatches mirrors her balance once again. (In making the proper decision, time is of the essence.)

Her perfumes are never blatant or even exotic. A fine scent, perhaps a Chanel or Bellodgia, something flowery but not oversweet, appeals to her. The Libra lady's sense of elegance is one part discreet, one part flirty insinuation, a combination of qualities purely opposite to her deepest sexual feelings.

The lady tends to enjoy foods that are extremely subtle in taste. She likes a little bit of everything, but it must be lovely, a real smorgasbord of flavors. Broccoli with butter sauce, veal *picatina*, dill flavorings, and lemon seasoning, for instance, pique her taste and imagination. She loves wine and is knowledgeable about the best years, the best vineyards, the finest chateaux. If you take her to dine, let her choose the wine.

Even simple vegetables like cabbage and cauliflower appeal to her if they're fresh—never frozen! The portions should be small and the seasoning subtle. She adores foods for their color as well, so the corn should be yellow, the cauliflower white, the green beans quite green. She absolutely craves foods imported from all over the world—a little bit of this or that often satisfying the inner Libra woman. It's the distilled essence of fine dining that most appeals to the Libra female. Graceful manners, an atmospheric setting, fine china, silver, white linen, and candlelight will make her appreciate you as well as the evening.

Where to Find Her

This lady is incredibly agreeable, ready and willing to work, before, during, and after marriage. She hates being alone, so she'll likely land a job to be with people actively engaged in some occupation.

Compatible with most situations, the Libra woman generally advances to high positions on the professional scale. Even if in disagreement, she prefers not to argue but to show you where and how you're wrong. They make great buyers for department stores, in notions, trinkets, or jewelry, and conversely, do very well as city employees or government workers. Their agreeable nature and the natural stimulus they find in work is more important than that which they experience in social functions. The Libra lady loves being in harmonious, intelligent company, even if it's just contributing to chitchat. And they're vigorous enough to enjoy it every night of the week if it's available. She's usually smiling and very pleasant to be around. A smart, cheerful appearance and friendly demeanor are bound to attract.

Librans do very well as hotel executives, able to smooth over complaints with devastating cool. If you sign up for symphony tickets, you won't be alone, because this girl will likely turn up beside you. Since they don't like to be alone, they'll attend musical functions with a girlfriend, a maiden aunt, or a co-worker. Anybody, somebody to share with.

A gardening club is a good spot to find a Libran, because she likes to share the discoveries of nature with others. The wonders of horticulture inspire her inquisitive, quick mind.

As to music, don't expect to find her playing in the orchestra. She probably wouldn't enjoy the constant pressure of perfecting a technique to play a musical instrument well. She'd rather join a music-appreciation class, learning about every aspect of the subject, including composers and conductors and what's new in the classical sphere.

Much of the time during class, those active eyes are scanning the students to see if there are any desirable men to meet. If she spots an appealing face, the dimples go headlong into a beautiful big smile, and her long lashes beat away, blinking the "I'd-like-to-meet-you" signals. Although she really means it, upon an approach you could see those same eyes open wide in wonderment: "Where did you come from, and who asked you here?"

Primary Move

Her actions sometimes deny what she feels within, because she does have an innate sense of what's proper and right, so if she's your quarry, the best way to meet her is to arrange an introduction through a friend. She's not at all priggish, but it's got to be done correctly, in tune with her sense of balance. She doesn't want to wake up accusing herself of being an easy mark.

After you meet, you might suggest a symphony concert where there'll be a new work by a new composer with innovative sounds. This appeals to her inquisitive sense. If you say you're going to pick her up at seven-thirty, be there on time, elegantly dressed. She has a great appreciation of a man who's attentive to his attire. A tuxedo or formal wear is not necessary, but you can be very acceptable in a well-cut conservative business suit with just the right amount of color and verve in your tie.

Have your car washed and shiny, treating her like Cinderella going to the ball as you lead her to the door and help her in.

Upon arrival at the theater, make sure your tickets agree with the seat numbers. Being disturbed by being improperly seated by an usher is your fault, not his. Every movement should be man-of-the-worldish. Sitting beside her, don't make the mistake of an overt or quick movement to handle her; rather, use words to admire those beautiful eyes, and subtly suggest a late dinner after the concert.

Make sure you pick the fanciest, most exquisite Continental or French restaurant. It's here you'll make your greatest impression, because this girl is attuned to sweet music and lovely surroundings as an integral part of her dining enjoyment.

Order something light, since it's late, nothing overly spicy or heavy with sauces. And ask her to order the wine if she professes her interest aloud. She may demur, but it's best if you insist that she do the selecting. Your admiration of her simplicity in dress, your optimistic and honest praise, will probably have her convinced by this time that you're all right, that you could have a lovely interlude together.

When it comes time to order the demitasse, she may throw you a clue to have it at her home, so grab it as you would a lifeline. You know she's not the type to be alone and is probably living with her family, which is a condition that might make it kind of difficult to get friendlier. But, come what may, things are going too well to let disappointment interfere now. You agree it would be marvelous to have coffee at her home.

She's a teaser, especially on her own home ground. Bright as can be, but she'll never let you know it. She'd rather be thought "beautiful but dumb." Her irresistible charm can be turned off or on at will.

The Libra woman is an incurable romantic. Her natural look takes her a long way. No wonder you find her so desirable; she's the incarnation of the all-American girl, the girl next door. In fact, everybody's mental picture of what a first love should be.

Call her bluff after demitasse, though, and discover if she's on or off; it's not easy to judge her mood. You never can tell with a Libran's nature which way the dice will fall, snake eyes or seven. But it's worth the gamble; you're making great strides. Speaking of strides, why not a short hike to the gazebo on the rise of that little hill? Whether it's summer, spring, fall, or winter, it's still a romantic spot, evoking memories of shy ladies, teatime, and unimportant chatter. A refuge of a sort. Set the scene for the "Sweetheart of Sigma Chi," and she'll assent to your romantic purpose.

Pre-coitus

With promises in her eyes, she'll hold your hand on the way to your tryst. She'll rub her thigh against yours and practically fall all over you as she conveniently stumbles on a rock. Oh, she's a tease; but patience, your day's coming, and soon. It's lovely there, best place to take her to see if she's really ready to come through. Fantasy flirting's O.K., but tonight is payoff time. Embrace her as you both look out over the night. There's one star twinkling its brilliance through the black and cloudy sky. She points to it, and like a little girl says, "Make a wish." Do it. Say it out loud. "I wish that this beautiful creature standing here beside me will . . ." (No, not "hop into bed with me." Be nice!) ". . . kiss me sweetly."

She giggles and replies, "That's an easy wish to make come true." Coolly turning her head to you, closing her eyes, and puckering her lips, she lifts her head to be kissed.

It has to occur to you that when you finally get her, you've just got to knock off this foolish flirting. It's all right to a point, but, c'mon, Libra lovely, get with it.

Impatient with her foolishness, you use more aggressiveness than you planned, catching her upper lip in your mouth and sucking it. A squeal comes, and then you feel her body relax. You can almost see the girly veneer dissipate, and this Lady Libra becomes the lusty, loving girl you imagined her to be. She tries like a pro, not an inexperienced amateur, to reach your lower teeth with her tongue. You keep her lip in your mouth while you run your tongue over her pink gums, tasting her.

"Where can we go, where can I touch your face and kiss your breasts and know everything about you?" Tough to do, but you manage somehow to speak with your eyes. Act II, scene 2, she guides you to the deserted hothouse and garden toolroom.

The warm and humid air in the greenhouse, along with the succulent odors of growing things, is a marvelous stimulant for all the senses. Life springing anew, seeds singing their song into the growth of leaves and buds and flowers. She's really blinking those eyes now, and not to be cute, but from ardent anticipation. Rather than stumble your way through the dark with no moonlight to show a path, hold her against the door of the tool shed while kissing her fingertips. Then take the palm of her hand, leading it down to touch the bulge caught between your legs. She's ready to dig, and places her hand over your tool, grasping it fervently, as anxious as you to know him better. Kiss her other hand, letting your tongue slip in between her fingers, guiding them to unzip your trousers. She clumsily extracts the spade from your pants, catching a hair on the zipper. She caresses the hurt spot and rubs your penis with her thumb, pressing harder against the tip. Pinching, tweaking, fretting it with both hands until you have to stop her or fun's done.

It's hot in the greenhouse, and as you hold your Libra's breast, you feel the dampness underneath. You forage down her dress to her belly button, dampness gliding your way. Reaching her birth dimple, you tamper and tickle it, which in turn excites her clitoris. Feeling her stomach contract under your palpating hand, you remove it from the top of her dress and reenter from beneath her skirt, to explore between her thighs. You can feel the exuberant dew drops trickling from her glowing cunt. You're already to take her on the dirt floor, but alas, Lady Libra has a better idea. Her forty-foot yacht at the dock, tethered tightly until the next trip, is easily available.

Hastily you zip your trousers, nudging your anxious penis back into your shorts as she adjusts her bosom back into her bra. Then, like two excited kids, you run like mad for the boat. In no time at all you're there.

The night is dark and tranquil as you climb aboard. In a few short seconds you've hoisted your anchor out of your pants, and all other clothes have gone portside on deck as you take each other in impatient desire.

Coitus

The hard deck is no purveyor of comfort, and the smell of varnish and antiseptic soap isn't jasmine and myrrh, but it makes no difference as you mate.

There's a wild and exultant feeling, copulating on deck, under the heavy cover of fog. As if wrapped in absorbent cotton, soundless, insulated from all harassment and concern. A splinter or two in your fanny are minor deterrents, a small price to pay for your Libran's love.

A lightning flash, and you ejaculate, causing a giant thrust from Libra's hips as she swims with you through the tidal wave.

The sea is calm, and you make your way to the cabin below. Time out now for a little medical attention as she takes her tweezers from her cosmetic kit, dabs the pincers with alcohol taken from the ship's stores, and proceeds to extract the wood slivers from your hindside. Her natural sense of humor takes precedence as she jokes every time you squeal. She enjoys your speedy recovery from surgery and is playful now.

The narrow bunk is invitingly intimate. So easy to roll over and dip in once again.

You find renewed thrills as she strokes your penis to its former degree of hardness. You find yourself ready, and once again you are thrusting deeper and deeper inside her. As the boat moves on its moorings, the natural drift and your meaningful motion finally have your Libra woman in orgasmic spasm.

She is a naturally lovely woman, and sheared of her veneer, a sensational sex partner who meets and surpasses all your preconceived daydreams.

Post-coitus

After resting awhile and talking quietly of places she'd like to visit, clothes she's seen and would love to buy, apartments with certain pieces she'd like to own, you find her slowly reverting to the tease. Throwing croquettish barbs as to how you could handle getting her those things. Don't let her kid you again. You know that under that dainty darling's lightweight talk there's a fiery Libra woman who does know what she wants.

A few tender kisses, and once again she's your woman. Lady Libra, whose only desire, really, is to couple with you.

SCORPIO (October 23– November 21)

The Scorpio Man

Recognition

The Scorpio male combines a secretive nature, inquisitive mentality, and true mysticism with down-to-earth practical ability. When it comes to sexual prowess, he's one of the most outstanding signs of the zodiac. He is usually the possessor of an energetic, thrusting personality. Usually medium in height, with a square face and a strong wide jaw, his size belies his great faculty for success and power.

His eyebrows are full and prominent, the sort one should be wary of, responding as a barometer to his expressive face. They move like punctuation marks. Exclamation points to question marks are indicative of the parade of thoughts crossing his mind.

His eyes are steady and piercing, gray, green, or brown, and when he focuses his attention, the recipient of his gaze definitely "feels" something. Whatever message he's sending is obvious by his eyes and eyebrows. Scorpio's nose is sometimes prominent, and usually aquiline, with a small bump. His hair is thick and more often than not is curly. Many Scorpio men have a reddish chestnut-color hair that grays late in life. Although his mouth is large, with a full lower lip, it's rarely droopy, giving a firm and positive impression that he really knows what he's talking about when he speaks. It's that light in his eyes, that intense and meaningful look of his, that people notice first.

The Scorpio physique is extremely well-proportioned, hard, and chunky, not prone to fat. Aside from his slim waist, there's nothing much to comment on except a trim, compact frame well put together and very wiry. His personality is powerful, and you can feel his presence in a room. Being quite emotional and creative, he rebels against restraints, a perfect target for reverse psychology. When you say "no" to him, that means "go." He must get things done, almost driven to achieve his goals. The Scorpio man makes things happen in his world, because he's sharp and shrewd and can read between the lines in most situations. He knows and senses things that evade others; it seems he can pull answers out of the ether. Possessed of great vitality, force, and energy, Scorpio can forge ahead where others would find the going heavy.

The Scorpio male is very critical. He fortifies himself by knowing everything, and in his opinion there's only one way to do anything, and that's his way. But first you can be sure he'll know the how, why, where, when, and what of all subjects he desires to deal with.

He's not exactly stubborn in the general sense. Scorpio is just very hard to influence. He's quite often like a time bomb ticking away until detonated. You'll recognize this in him by his nervous qualities, perhaps a facial tic, a swinging leg, a doodling habit, or that annoying sound of cracking knuckles. He's outspoken, very often tactless and cutting. Perhaps of all the signs, the Scorpio is the man who really couldn't give a damn about what "they" think.

Mentally, he's logical, calculating, and intuitive, and comes equipped with built-in foresight. Sometimes his overly optimistic judgment eggs him on too soon, forcing him to plunge where none of his associates are prepared to venture forth.

Sexually, he can become passionate at the blink of an eye or the snap of a finger. In fact, that's his one major problem. He's usually impetuous, all for the momentary pleasure of sex, and if he does experience a downfall in life, it quite often can be attributed to his zealous appetite, sometimes very indiscriminate. Then, all at once, his dreams vanish, his castles crumble, due to some irate husband or beleaguered boyfriend. Frankly, the needs of his penis can overcome his other excellent qualities of judgment. At the wiggle of a hip, he's a stud ready to mount. If it's a little hard to get, he likes it better, spurning the too-easy conquest, whether it involves business, hobbies, sports, or women.

The Scorpio plays games in his personal relationships. The one-upmanship sort of thing. He usually finds it difficult to deal with an open, frank friendship. There is then created by him an intriguing undercurrent that is felt and hard to define. You may know him—or think you do—for fifty years, and still not fully understand him.

When it comes to clothes, he's like a mannequin, dapper and compact. He'll tend to a variety of conservative colors, but not the cut. He's the sort of man who would affect spats if they were in fashion. His pants will fit like a second skin, particularly around the pelvis area. Shirts, often custom-made, are fitted to his body to perfection. Scorpio, under casual conditions, will open his shirt above his navel and tie the tails in a knot to look dashing and smart. But in business clothes, he's sharp, good-looking, and shrewdly dressed in a blue or brown suit, contemporary or very mod cut, but always slick and well-groomed. He has the know-how to dress for the sort of people he's seeing at the moment; like a chameleon, he changes color and clothes and controls his personality.

He's not much for jewelry, fancying tourmalines or opals, and like the Libran, not hoodwinked by the supposedly evil spirit attached to these gems. He'll wear them and buy them as gifts for others.

The Scorpio man particularly puts down hexes, voodoo spells, and the like. Perceptive and deeply psychic, he refrains from accepting such "childishness." But you'll find him knocking on wood, throwing salt over his left shoulder, and avoiding black cats.

His tastes in food are totally unorthodox and a part of his inconoclastic being. The Scorpio's a prime stud and is likely to believe that certain foods are highly aphrodisiac. Although these beliefs are the result of old wives' tales and without valid proof after years of experimentation by nutritionists, he's still convinced it's so. The intake of such foods has no physiological effect whatever, but you just can't convince him of this. What he's really moved by are the senses—the smell, taste, and beautiful presentation of certain food. He's thoroughly positive, as most male Scorpios are, that such items as oysters, asparagus, eggs, onions, garlic, and of all things, vanilla, will encourage his sexual longevity and versatility.

He enjoys whiskey, because he likes a drink and, naturally, assumes liquor makes a twosome sexier.

Don't be finicky about food with Scorpio. He loves almost everything—thick soups, dark bread, southern Italian food, Spanish peasant food—and he is likely to accent it all with pepper (black, green, red, or cayenne) and any hot sauce available. His taste for spices is beyond belief. Here again, he thinks that hot seasoning makes a hot, hot Scorpio!

If you try too hard to figure him out, you'll only find yourself going in circles. His facility to seem outgoing and frank about all things is a delusion. The real facts, the real man, the real truth, are all his own information, all of which is forever part and parcel of his deeply secretive nature.

Where to Find Him

Some of the world's most successful con men, used-car salesmen, home-improvement experts, and fund raisers are Scorpios. He's a complex composition of the turn-on artist and lover of the world's humanity.

This fascinating man is so sexually virile that he's compatible (because of his own desire) with all other signs of the zodiac. Most Scorpio males are marvelously intelligent, interested in benefiting mankind, and not just sexually. He's the sort who could turn minerals into a chemical that could end the energy crisis. You could find him deeply engrossed in an experiment, laboriously testing time after time after time to come up with the proper cure for a disease or to perfect a product for human consumption. He has the tenacity to go on and on until he achieves his goals. He's very adept at uncovering mysteries in the field of research and practical science.

Scorpio makes a great builder—not just a few houses or a building or two, but whole towns and communities. His vision is large. Tiny ripples are neither significant nor worthwhile to him. It's the big circles, the great challenges, the universe to conquer. The mental picture of a whole town growing out of a barren desert or a swamp is like a "high" for him. He sees the people moving about, shopping, swimming, golfing—living. Children going to schools he built, students using his libraries and gyms. He has a secret vision that is often incomprehensible to many. This, too, is part of his magnetism.

A naval career is not out of the ordinary for Scorpio. His affinity for water could be the attraction, but invariably it's the travel "Navy" implies. The strange cities and ports throughout the world excite his imagination. The many mysteries to be investigated in foreign countries. The people to know, their mannerisms, customs, and way of life. And their women!

He also makes a very successful policeman or detective and usually climbs to the top of the heap in this profession. Work of this nature offers satisfaction to several facets of his needs—unraveling mysteries, being his own man, and helping humanity in a way that is not mundane but full of surprises and change.

Conversely, many of the most notorious criminals are Scorpios. That need of one-upmanship, trying to outsmart the other guy. The excitement and edginess of crime. All aspects of the Scorpio man's complexities could be fulfilled in walking that vague line between right and wrong, playing it for the full thrill of "not getting caught."

Again, conversely, they make excellent trust officers in the banking world, and you can't top them as auctioneers. They know a bargain when they see one, and can sell it. Or at a carnival, you must win if you bet at least three out of five pitchmen are Scorpios.

Outdoor sports requiring stratagems capture the Scorpio male. Watching football and calling the quarterback's plays is his main entertainment in viewing the game. Great strategists, they can sit over a chessboard all day and give the champions great competition.

As for hobbies, anything dealing with the occult, magic, or witchcraft will entice him into years of investigation. Although he claims he doesn't believe in any of it, that he's just a psychic investigator, time could and usually does prove he's kidding himself. He frowns on the fact that people believe that hexes and other spells exist, but mention you've come across a centuries-old recipe for a "love potion" and watch his eyes—they'll show his thrill at the thought. He'll be stimulated to the extreme.

Primary Move

To bed the Scorpio male, your only problem is where. Usually his apartment is equipped to handle all sorts of unexpected as well as expected visits. A phone call will do it. Use his involvement in the psychic-investigation realm as the key. He's a doer. He's the man of the week, the year, the cen-

The Lovers' Guide to Sensuous Astrology

tury, when it comes to sex and love. Move in fast; his auctioneer's perception will quickly size up what's happening. You don't have to spell S-E-X out for the Scorpio to get the idea, but remember, he doesn't go for too easy a pushover, so use your head as well as your eyes and body when they say "come hither."

Preparation on your part is minimal. Dress casually; the right heady perfume always helps. His nature is such that he's ready to make a meaningful pass simultaneously with your entrance. Cool him off with witty conversation and heat him up with innuendos. Tell him you've been wanting to show him that ancient excerpt about an easily concocted love potion. Make a copy of it by hand, equating the materials and ingredients available on today's market. Needless to say, once you've got him thinking and stimulated, a trip to the nearest herb shop and a supermarket will be in the offing. Cooking together, measuring properly, and laughing it up while you do so should impress him greatly.

Once the potion is prepared, a shot glass full of the brew should do the trick. Psychologically he's naturally prepared for it to work, and really that's exactly what you've been after.

Waiting now is no hardship, although you are hopeful he'll make the usual expected overtures. You're in for a surprise!

Pre-coitus

None.

Coitus

Oddly enough, there's no true pre-sex-play with the Scorpio man. Fondling, touching, and kissing are not particularly interesting to him. His ardor requires no stimulant. His inner force of nature arouses him, at any moment, at any time.

He has a flexible but proved routine that is adaptable to many occasions. So if you find yourself at a loss as to why he's disrobing unconcernedly, don't ask! If you watch, you can see his signals as he casually slips off his shoes and socks, removes his shirt, hops out of his trousers, and seats himself in an easy chair.

He's so relaxed, so sure of himself. So positive his casual undressing sort of shocked you. He's a wily one and knows his women. Talk about psychological advantages, he knows every game in the book. He's eyeing you with a half-smile. Not a come-hither expression, but a challenge. "What now?" A dare. "O.K., I'm all yours."

But you are stunned; you don't know what to think.

It's really a funny sight, seeing him there. You envision an Indian chief's bonnet of feathers on his head. If it weren't for his impish smile, you might expect to see a war dance. He's hot, and he wants you to know it.

He still sits there, masculine legs spread, body relaxed, his penis resting for the moment like a warrior home on furlough. He's waiting for your move. Approach him as if on an errand of great importance. He's sent his signals and now waits for your move. Slowly, his penis will awaken, growing to its magnificent proportions. Greet his penis, openly marveling at the size, devour whole the firmness while sucking in your cheeks and coursing your tongue over him.

Surprised at your aggressive attack, but nonetheless delighted, he'll let you continue. In fact, urge you on your fling.

Remove his penis from your mouth and ask him to lift his legs high enough on the chair so that his scrotum is no longer hiding that tender place beneath. Take little nips with your teeth there and massage his ready penis as you do so. Pull the curly black hairs with your lips, and bite harder. Scorpio is really at a loss for words. Those sounds you hear are unleashed passion he's never known before.

This is just for starters. You're off and running in a race destined to be a win with no handicap.

He's been somewhat passive, just reacting. Now he takes the reins. He knows the track—muddy, clear, dry, or otherwise. He's ridden this turf before, and the odds are always in his favor. Tonight it looks as though it's going to be a dead heat. You don't mind; you're betting with him, not against him.

Gallantly he disrobes you. Faster than you believed possible, you'll be divested of all clothing but your panties. Where he developed this technique so dexterously isn't hard to imagine. "Experience is the mother of invention" is the way he quotes it, and there's the answer to your query.

The Scorpio man will stand back with his hypnotically intense eyes. As if by psychokinesis, your bikini-T-string will move over your hips and fall like a fluttering leaf to the floor.

Step high, out of them, and walk sensuously toward him. Move your body, signaling him on as he did you. Remember,

The Lovers' Guide to Sensuous Astrology 119

it took him most of the evening to get this far, so, you've played hard to get, now give in.

A moment ago he just sat there, legs apart. Copy him. Stand there in his fashion. Surprise! You expect cunnilingus. Uh-uh, not from him. The Scorpion never does what's most obviously expected or appropriate.

He'll lead you into the bathroom and into the tub. You expect it'll happen now! No. He'll place you against the wall with the feel of cold tile on your back and tell you to grasp the towel bar behind your head. Satisfied you're in proper position, he'll tell you he'll be right back.

"He's mad, perhaps. But if this is insanity, let me rave!" you'll think to yourself.

When Scorpio returns, he's armed with a seltzer bottle filled with champagne and announces you're about to experience a gourmand's delicacy, the Sunshine Shower.

And so, your body tense and waiting, he steps into the bathtub, stands about three feet away facing you, and commences to shower you with the golden liquid. And the sun-kissed grapes never had it so good, rolling in little streamlets between and on your breasts, under and along your hips, on top of and behind your thighs.

Since he's most appreciative of aphrodisiac food and drink, your body offers him a chef's masterpiece. Liquid light nectar, glistening on your taut skin. Your trembling body is itself, a banquet. And he begins to feast.

Looking at and lapping each drop. Then dipping his tongue tenderly underneath your breasts without touching them with his hands. He dawdles awhile at the nipples, then removes the squirter from the bottle and slowly pours champagne over your gleaming mounds. He lets it drip in his mouth, and as he laps it up, he catches your nipples with his upper lip each time he goes for more.

He strains the heady brew from your drenched pubic hairs, holding your vulva closer to his mouth to catch the wine. He lets his tongue test to see if there's more between your lips. He continues to explore all the hot places that may still hold some champagne. He vigorously sucks to get it all. Scorpio, a true lover of the grape.

Then, feeling and finding your wetness even more appealing than he anticipated, he seats you in the tub and lies between your parted legs, holding his mouth right under your vagina. The Scorpion pours the balance of champagne from the bottle, letting it shower over your dewy patch and trickle in a small delicious stream onto his tongue. He's lost himself in the wondrous world of the grape and you.

The bacchanal continues on the bathroom floor. You're on your knees (in such a small place, this position is most appropos), arms extended, supporting your body doggie-style, eyeing the serial number on the bathroom scale.

More of the Sunshine Shower has rivuleted between your cheeks ... ah, he missed there. Onward! He's determined you know and will continue to explore every crack and cranny until all's been lapped up.

Wet with sunshine drops, enhanced with pungent body mist, the treasure trove, your anxious jewel box, is ready to be looted.

That Scorpio man is a pirate. Like Bluebeard, he's intent on stealing the goods. His trusty penis, keyed up for action, enters your cave and finds its way to your exquisite total surrender. He shifts his shaft once more, and you explode as he ejaculates in perfect unison with your orgasm.

Post-coitus

What a mysterious fellow, so giving, so full of unexpected devious pranks in sex, and now ... done. Really done, as if it never were. He's like a finely tuned instrument, sensational when in use, when finished, totally done, finis! But he'll tuck you under his arm like a newspaper, yesterday's news, perhaps. At least you're not discarded!

He has such a highly sexual nature that his mind works overtime sending signals to his genitals. Although he won't gloat about his past, in a male bull session his percentages of wins has to be at least forty-five percent higher than any other sign in the zodiac. Too bad this virile Scorpion can't savor the difference between his skirmishes and realizes he's not always the conquering hero. He does have fun, though, and can renew his relationship with you four weeks ahead just as if he were with you the night before.

He's like a wandering minstrel keeping womanhood happy with his unique service.

He'll be warm and friendly, start scheming right out about a deal he's consummating, and as an afterthought: "What's on your schedule a week from next Tuesday?" You see, that gives him more than a week and a half to try other tracks. You can be sure he won't be sitting in the bleachers or clubhouse. He'll be down where the action is. Who knows, this time it was the Sunshine Shower, next trip with Scorpio it could be the Silver Stirrup. What's that?

Like it or not, that's his way, and if you want him, play your bets according to the tote board.

The Scorpio Woman

Recognition

The Scorpio woman is to many the total female—passionate, glamorous, exciting, a vertiable wow! Her face is never quite beautiful, but, oh, is it fascinating. There's something enticing about the bone structure and the piercing eyes, which can be green, gray, brown, any color. Her stare is decidedly compelling, looking at and through you like an X-ray machine. She may appear frosty at times, but even the most unresponsive person feels a tingle or two when around this female. She exudes sex, not just in her involvement with men, but in the very wonder and splendor of her being. Her sign rules the generative organs, the pelvis area, and it shows. She reflects delight, wonder, and fulfilled promise.

Her nose might have an appealing little bump, and the nostrils are attractive. She exhibits a luscious fullness in her lower lip, this Scorpio lady, never pouting, but showing uninterest, total proof that she has no feeling for the conventional or what others think of her. Her high cheekbones mark her as an excellent model; the jaw is wide and very severe in cut, supporting angular facial planes. Her rather fullish neck is neither slender nor particularly feminine, but she's a clever camouflage artist, ever playing down her liabilities. The average Scorpio female is of medium height, seldom tending to fat. Most are quite often slender, but even the most buxom usually have well-proportioned figures and firm breasts. Eyebrows are prominent, and Scorpio pays great attention to shaping, because they could be overpowering on the face. She has a trick of making them an incredibly exciting frame for the eyes.

Her complexion is most usually dusky, a burnished olive with hair shaded anywhere from light brunette to brown with red highlights. Her eccentricities of living often have her bleaching or tinting her hair red, and it's usually very curly. A lot of Scorpio women will have their hair straightened as a cosmetic device, and love to indulge in beauty treatments.

She uses body language, this one. When you spot her walking, you can tell her sign by the way she moves her hips. She says, literally, "You're mine, I possess you," or "I don't care," or "Don't approach me," or even, "Watch yourself." With a flick of a hip or a leg movement she can create an entire conversation, even while sitting. The Scorpio uses her body instead of words. A secretive personality herself, she tends to draw from others all their secrets, even family skeletons, yet her secrets are very much her own. She's forceful and dominating and will do anything and everything to achieve her ends, while affecting a kindly help-the-world attitude, too.

Once you're hers, it's total consumption with the Scorpio. Even if you get the urge to stray now and then, if you're loving to her and always sexy, she'll keep her peace. After all, once in a while isn't always. Scorpio is easy to anger, compulsive, sarcastic, cutting, and passionate. There naturally has to be a jealousy to match, and she's prone to imagine what really doesn't exist at all, so watch it!

She has a "don't-cage-me" attitude and strong desire for freedom, so let her go on a long leash. She won't disappear. She just has to feel she's free. She can outmaneuver almost anyone, but in a highly intelligent, honest way. If she has to be destructive, she will. Scorpio is all female, no holds barred, and usually gets what she wants.

Her clothes have a flair, a bright, brilliant look that results in excitement, color and drama. She'll wear any new fashion that will best exhibit that figure, and likes sheer blouses, the no-bra look, being first to display herself provocatively. She has a passion for mixed colors and wild combinations of red, pink, and green; blue, orange, and white; or, on the opposite end of things, she can be utterly conservative at times, depending on her mood. She can make tweeds look sexy, and appear cool and aloof in tailored clothes. Anything goes. It's not the clothing, it's the way she expresses the cut and fabric with her body.

Her flair extends to hats, turbans, and scarves. Her perfumes will be decidedly provocative, no flowery or subtle scents, but blatant and exciting nostril twitchers. Jewelry is very important here, too.

Paradoxically, as a youth she inclines to appear older, and as she ages, tends to be younger in appearance. You just can't keep up with the Scorpio woman. So hypersexual is she that she overdoes in other fields, most notably smoking and sometimes drinking. Her changeable tendencies extend to her looks, where for months at a time she will appear vibrant, alive, Miss Come-and-get-it. Then, suddenly, she'll have a sad look in her eyes and a passive rather than vibrant manner. However, no matter what her mood, she always looks desirable.

She loves food, particularly the pungent, heavy variety, like sharp cheese, oysters, escargots, garlic, onions, dark bread, Mexican dishes, olives, eggs, and spices. She finds sexual pleasure in the phallic shape of asparagus, celery, and carrots.

This sexpot will nibble at flowers because of their sometimes exotic flavor, and when it comes to liquor, no fancy ladies' cocktails for her. Give her unadulterated drinks, but watch that she doesn't overindulge. Many Scorpions like that fast, neat feeling that comes with a straight shot, that come-and-get-me atmosphere that's created by Scotch, rye, or bourbon. But even then, she'll fool you with a frosty exterior. It doesn't mean a thing; she's a good actress all the way.

Where to Find Her

If it's Scorpio you want, you've got a tiger by the tail. She's always involved in activities requiring maximum mental effort. She's aggressive, down-to-earth, cold, and calculating when need be, but possessed of a great understanding of her fellow man. Her perceptiveness lies not in psychic ability, but in her X-ray vision. You'll find her in any of the scientific fields, perhaps in research; she may be a laboratory technician or functioning as an expert surgeon. The Scorpio female makes an exceptionally fine mathematician, bank officer, or lawyer, and excels in any field that can benefit from her computerlike mind. She'd make a whiz as comptroller, might even be attracted to archaeology, either in museum research or actual digging.

For fun, she enjoys skiing because it involves that fantastic body of hers. Fashion shows would benefit from her presence, and even if something she wears is not particularly to your liking, she'll make it look good. You'll find her on a ladies' baseball or basketball team, and percentage-wise, she's heavy on the tennis court. In court or in bed, she's full of the love of life and remains ever involved.

Primary Move

No quickie dates for her. Secrecy and mystery excite her. Plan an all-day affair, but keep your plans a surprise. Be firm, very masculine, and if you make a date for ten A.M., be there. Give her an idea of what to wear—sneakers, shorts, tennis dress, what-have-you, because she'll need them. If tennis is the game, let her have it, because if she wins (or you let her win) you're lost and can simply forget the rest of the day. If you're the winner, then you're king and can call the other shots. It's time for a snack, so forget the fancy restaurants and take her to a seafood place with a clam bar. She'll get a sexual thrill out of oysters or clams and the ceremony of opening the shells with a knife slipped between the lips of the shell. Steer the conversation toward archaeology, the universe, or even her version of where Atlantis lost itself, and casually slip in the news that you've a six-thirty surprise that will delight her. Deliver her home for freshening up—not yours, it's much too soon. Titillate her, make her itch a bit. For the evening's pleasure, find a good medium, palmist, fortune-teller, or astrologer, pick Ms. Scorpio up promptly, and she'll more than likely be wearing a caftan, turban, and long beads, all set for the mystic occasion. After the reading (which by the way will involve a delightful new man in her life), suggest a midnight supper in a little Italian place with exotic dishes, highly spiced and served with a basic Chianti or house wine, or even sangría. After supper, you'll have no trouble taking it—and her—from there.

Pre-coitus

None

Coitus

There are no preliminaries with the vivacious, hypersexual Scorpio woman. She needs sex as one needs water to survive. Her libido is strong, greater than a Moonchild could possibly imagine. Her seductive walk and serpentine movements are in contrast to her cool-looking beauty. That gnawing in her groin that's ever present needs daily fulfillment.

To find her satisfied after lovemaking, one must be acquainted with all the subtleties of sexual technique. Unless experience and super technique are manifested, there's every possibility that after being with you she could arrange an even later date.

It's position in life that's important to the Scorpio woman, and I don't mean "social." You'd better work out in the gym, do your calisthenics and deep-breathing exercises regularly and watch your diet. Be trim and in top form to prepare yourself properly for your encounter with the Scorpio seducer.

An arrangement in advance to whet her appetite isn't necessary. If you've struck home, and you should on your primary move, get ready for action immediately.

Alone now in her apartment, conversation and witty remarks are meaningless. It's what you do, not what you say that's sure-fire. Press her to you, clasping the back of her head in your hand, the other arm around her waist. Take tiny bites of her ear, just nippy enough to feel great, but don't draw blood. Kiss the other ear, inserting your tongue into the tiny crevice, whispering passionate words of love and seduction. Real low-down language won't shock her.

A moan will escape her lips. She's with it and probably has already had an orgasm. Tease her, cut her lower lip with your teeth, sharply enough so the whole mouth quivers. Drawing your hand from her hair, pull your fingernails ever so lightly against her throat. Place your hand on her breast, squeezing, harder than usual. Dig your nails in gently around the outer diameter of her aureole, leaving red crescent moons on her skin. Then plunge your lips to the wounded spot and suck voraciously.

She's been waiting for you, and this welcome meeting may never end. Being a sexy wanton, she'll pull away, smiling lasciviously. Removing her clothes and asking you to do the same, she guides you to her bedroom. Why not play the main event in the arena?

Once there, all your preparations during the past month come into play. You'll need strength, prowess, and dynamic control to handle this hot piece.

Lean against a wall where there's a long expanse of space. Get a firm grip on the rug with your feet. Pull her to you, putting your hands under her buttocks. Tell her that when you press up on her derriere, she should lift her hips, placing her legs around your waist, and brace her feet against the wall. You're pressing and nothing happens, as if she didn't hear you. You follow her gaze and discover she's mesmerized by the size of your penis. She stands there staring at it, as if never having seen anything so imposing before. Just for a moment your ego soars, and so it should! Back to business. When this position is accomplished, your friends can call you Hercules. Pinch her bottom and again repeat your instructions. Tell her she's going to "Nail Him," which is the name of your little game.

Grasp her tightly, for now you penetrate her to the hilt, and this is it. Really what she's been waiting for. To participate properly in this position, she must move and you must hold her securely. Tell her to rock forward and back, pressing and releasing, back and forth. Oh, she catches on fast. Once moving, you find the easiest way to keep your balance and let her manage the movement. Another moaning sound, and there she goes again. A long whistling sound as air escapes between her teeth. Her vagina shudders, grasping your enflamed organ tighter. More, and she rocks. More, and she socks it to you. If you can handle it, and want to play some, start howling like a wolf at the moon. The masculine voice loudly calling goes back to some prehistoric part of herself, sending eerie shivers throughout her body.

When the time comes and your knees feel as if they'll give way or that your arms will come out of their sockets from her weight, it's time to change position.

Down she goes, kind of wobbly herself. Take a break. Walk to the bed and toss her on it. This very brief respite should assure continued astonishment for our sensuous Scorpio. Remember, you're dealing with an insatiable appetite,

The Lovers' Guide to Sensuous Astrology

and that control you developed is like a blue-chip stock about to pay dividends.

She's lying on her back. Eyes shining, wondering what's coming. The secretive part of her nature appreciates this charade. Just a hint at a time, a sexual mystery for her to unravel. She'll find the proper clues as you kneel over her body in an upright position. Place her left foot on your shoulder, the other leg lying flat on the bed. This time you officiate, working your way carefully into her hot and anxious pussy, feeling your way, then tumble him in like a runaway train.

When he hits the end of the line, stop. Stay awhile, and depart. Try again. Meanwhile, her arms are flying wildly in the air, her body writhing in incredible, delicious pain.

Once again the "New York Express" gets on the tracks and tunnels through. Keep it up until you feel yourself coming. Still engulfed in her vagina, take down the left foot and grab her other ankle, lifting her right foot to your shoulder.

Try now, but go carefully. You don't want any neighbors banging on the door in response to her frantic cries.

Now she'll be moaning in a loud and lusty voice at your expertise, babbling that you must never leave her and this *is* what she's been waiting for.

After all, maybe you're Samson, but you're not a machine. Now it's your turn to become verbal as your orgasm explodes, seeming to last indefinitely. You and she will collapse in near-exhaustion.

But "near" is not complete! This is a night to remember. You're both allowed to rest awhile, say ten or fifteen minutes or so, because position number three has got to astound her. Again, it'll require her cooperation and ability to follow instructions.

If you wonder why she's so quiet, she's marveling at these imaginative positions she's performing. Never before has her ardor been so completely quenched in sex, and here ... you're ready to go again.

It's merry-go-round time, and you're going to play carrousel. She climbs on your rod while you're lying on your back. Lifting herself just enough so that two inches of your penis are exposed. Then, testing gingerly at first, she moves around on him in a complete circle. If she experiments a little, the Scorpio woman will quickly learn the most efficient manner in which to perform her assigned task. You see, the best part is, if she falls off the pony, the belting bronco just catches the golden ring again, and round and round she goes.

Dizzy with love, she lies flat on your stomach. Your stallion is running a fast trot, and Scorpio keeps her seat. As he gallops, she responds, and the success of the night is at hand. She screams . . . *enough!*

On this cue your penis spurts all over himself, her, and you.

Post-coitus

Unless there's some frightful hormone imbalance, her activities should be curtailed for a while. She's snuggling close, talking a blue streak about how each "trick" blew her mind. How well you instructed her, and on and on she goes. You're ready for sleep. To quiet her, stroke her clitoris, but gently if you aren't ready for another onslaught. Just stroke it as you would comfort anyone else by stroking their forehead or rubbing their back.

Soon she'll sleep. Well and long, looking like a little girl now, all innocence and virtue. But look closer; there's a little turned-up grin at the corners of her mouth. She's smiling in her sleep; and even in slumber, she's moving her hips a little in sensuous remembering. Don't disturb her. If you so desire, leave. But better yet, stay until morning. She'll sleep as close as your skin all night, and when the sun has been up for a few hours, she'll wake up, roll over, and say with her eyes still half-closed, "Hey, let's Nail Him!"

SAGITTARIUS
(November 22–December 21)

The Sagittarius Man

Recognition

The Sagittarius male is usually tall and slender and well-proportioned. He has a beautiful stride, never jagged or uneven in his bearing, and exudes dynamism and excitement when he moves. His head is beautifully shaped, with a long or oval face and rounded forehead. You can usually spot the Sagittarian by the way he holds his head, a bit to the side, expression always alert to what's going on around him or listening to what you have to say. They're rabid talkers, too. They abhor criticism, particularly that which is unwarranted.

The nose is generally aquiline, with a high bridge in a face that is quite attractive and never too large. His hair ordinarily will be wavy and brown through all the shades to chestnut.

Sagittarian's mouth is marvelous and moves with great flexibility. It's bowed, well-proportioned, with a long upper and lower lip, never overly full or sensual, but from these mouths come interesting conversation, fascinating tidbits, great gossip, and profound knowledge.

The ears are a bit large but well-proportioned and close to the face. The chin will slope, not in a weak sense, but the angle is quite pertinent to the character. His eyes are alert and always roving. Whether it's a good-looking woman passing or the net worth on a balance sheet, he's quick to catch any topic and make it part of his memory bank. The color of his eyes varies from blue to hazel to brown. No matter the color, they have a striking effect on people. Not so much hypnotic, but demanding one to stop, look, and listen.

The Sagittarian will have long legs made for walking and allowing for that gazellelike stride. He is great for outdoor sports, especially jogging. In fact, anything physical that will keep him in trim is O.K. He's got good muscles and square shoulders, and to keep such a build requires a great deal of exercise. You never can judge a Sagittarian's weight. They generally look lighter than they actually are. Those extra pounds are hard muscle. If he's a businessman with limited time, he'll still find an hour for a workout at the gym.

The Sagittarian is loving and definitely wants to please. He has an effusive personality and appreciates freedom. Because of his very independent and self-reliant personality, he's miserable if he's not his own boss. Most Sagittarians are either in business for themselves or work on their own in a large company. They're self-propelled, and time clocks would be a disaster. They dislike taking orders from others unless they fully respect their superior's mental achievements. They're honest, direct, and friendly in all issues. Although they're not mean personally, their comments can be sharp, tactless, and to the point. They are an ambitious lot, and one can usually depend on their first-sight analysis of people. When they're angry, watch out! The most obvious example of their temper is exhibited when they're unjustly accused of something they were supposed to have done or said. The fur can really fly. Cold, steely eyes; sharp-pointed tongue; a dart to the gut, a click of the heels, and they're gone. The recipient is often in shock and at a loss for words. Don't kid them about their looks, because that's their soft spot and they don't like personal criticism.

In the area of clothing, Sagittarians are casual but always neat. Since they're outdoorsy, they'll affect sport coats, shirts, and slacks; or the more costume look of Norfolk jackets and safari shirts. They hate to go the cleaners, so most of their wardrobe will be wash-and-wear, permanent press, and you'll find this man happily doing his duty at the local laundromat. He doesn't mind, because every article of clothing must be kept in perfect condition. He will not tolerate the smallest stain or the tiniest speck of lint. The Sagittarian more than likely will stick to deep olives, dark greens, or warm earth colors like topaz and sienna, which suggest earthy masculinity. His shoes will be fashionable, but comfort is the first requisite.

After-shaving scents are generally not his bag. He'll use none at all, or possibly a light skin bracer. He doesn't need this. His personality is a knockout; he's terribly exciting and can cause your imagination to run wild.

He's daring about food, and loves such exotic repasts as flambéd duck and lobster thermidor, and likes to experiment with the unknown. Conversely, he'll crave meatloaf if it's dolled up with odd herbs and spices. He enjoys the simplicity of fresh fruit, but doesn't go for overly odorous cheeses. When it comes to health foods, look out, because he's diet-conscious and will be fanatic for one month or so and then forget it. Heavy desserts are his nemesis. His strong willpower doesn't help when it's sweets time. He goes for the unusual in vegetables, seeking out items like artichokes, prickly pears, and avocados. Equal to an interest in eating different foods, he relishes the history of them, where they're grown or how they're manufactured, what kind of people eat them! Since he's interested in oddball cuisine, he's naturally great at preparing complicated dishes, but really has to be in the mood or it becomes a chore for him.

Because he's such an ebullient, effervescent character, he scarcely requires or desires alcohol as a stimulant, but is a whiz at mixing for others.

Where to Find Him

That distinctive gait generally serves as immediate recognition of the Sagittarian. You might find him headed toward a lecture podium, because Sagittarians are usually great speakers on almost any given matter. They're the type who become experts on an interesting subject in no time flat. They're also very successful in show business, so if you join a little-theater group, you're very likely to bump into all manner of Sagittarians.

This guy loves to travel, and doesn't mind going alone, because his open, friendly ways always attract people to talk to and enjoy. Las Vegas is a good spot to find him, because he has the gambling urge (for fun only, usually). He likes the color, excitement, and glamour of the players themselves and the flamboyant surroundings, and he'll risk a buck or two when he can afford it.

At a musical comedy or ballet, your Sagittarian will surface most prominently; some of them even study ballet themselves to preserve the poise and grace they feel they require for daily life.

They're interested in every sort of communications medium and the techniques of public relations and advertising. Television, radio, and movie making—all are suited to him. You'll rarely find these gentlemen patiently painting a picture or doing needlepoint. Archaeology fascinates them—exploration, looking for the unknown and undiscovered, not so much for the mystery of it, but for the excitement of seeking and finding.

The Sagittarius man hates to be cooped up, preferring a large home instead of a small house or apartment. When he can afford it, a large place to live is one of his indulgences. This wide-wide-world feeling takes him outdoors to enjoy just about any active sport.

If you take a writing course, you're likely to find this man, because he's an expert at crisp, informative business letters or commercial copywriting.

The Sagittarian is idealistic in his thinking, but he's extremely practical when it comes to his occupation. He has the facility to combine his innermost spirit with his business, and will succeed in startling you when he invites you to a lecture on "Self-Knowledge in This Level of Karma" after you've given in to one of his requests (even though you were dead set against it). He's some guy.

The unusual strikes a chord with the Sagittarius man, although he can accept the mundane. If you create an odd and new situation, he'll turn on to it fast. For instance, there's hardly anything more exciting for him than to be invited to your apartment to bake bread together! That's right—bake, not break. His fascination with origins of foods puts you in the prime position of sharing this interest by suggesting it; and who bakes bread today? He'll like that! But be sure you know what you're doing. Once you've got him to agree—and it shouldn't be difficult—go shopping and find the perfect pan, the right oils, the flour, yeast, and other ingredients. Then research the cooking procedure and practice until you're perfect. Your friends and neighbors should get a bang out of all the fine bread you're passing around. Talk about it first, go into each step in depth, and you'll really fascinate him.

You need no introduction with the Sagittarius male. Just walk right up and tell him you think he'd enjoy such an evening, and add that you love company. In other words, drop by, and he will!

Put an apron on him and let him participate. He won't mind taking instructions the first time. When the heavenly odor of baking bread fills your apartment and it's done to a turn, serve a snack. Toss a fresh vegetable salad with an unusual dressing that includes avocados. Have lots of pure, whipped creamery butter to put on your special bread. By the time you serve dessert, something rich and luscious, you'll have won him over.

While dining, talk about the newest religious cults in California, some intimate, interesting experiences you've had in the world of the psyche, and how your own psychic ability frightens you because you don't fully understand it. Since he's ready to tackle the unusual in any predicament, he'll put you at ease. It's his gambling spirit, and he'll try anything new. He acts out of instinct. So as the evening progresses, he'll get the idea very clearly when you feel you want to play house with him.

But take care. The Sagittarian is not a guy who'll play for keeps, and will shy away from overly romantic involvements or from anything he considers a sticky wicket. On the other hand, he'll remain a close and very loyal friend.

Don't suggest doing the dishes in front of this guy. Ask him to prepare you an after-dinner cordial and then let your own desires take it from there, because you've got him hooked.

Since the evening has been a great success, suggest a picnic for the following Sunday. On a farm where you spent a couple of weeks not too long ago. You're on, girl—food, nature, and you. What else could he ask for?

Pre-coitus

A day in the sun, open fields, and growing crops stir the spirit. Mother earth is a fecund place, and a farm, well-tended, is inspirational to the inner core of man. The planting of seeds, nurturing by water and sun, maturing, then harvest.

The Sagittarian is having a ball. His busy afternoon in the great outdoors, free as the milkweed floating in the breeze, is what makes him happy. He's with all of nature. This is great, but tiring, and human needs for water must be tended to.

Ah, there's a barn. A storage place for hay to feed the

horses. And, see, munching cows nearby, udders no longer swollen with milk, but long and phallic-looking.

A tremor runs through his penis as he watches the pastoral scene. The day has developed an earthy sense of well-being, but his other needs seem in want of satisfaction, too.

You're a wily one to plan a day like this for your sagacious Sagittarian. He playfully races you to the barn, stopping at the well. Pumping on the handle, you drink from the tin cup and are refreshed by the cold spring water.

Although it's his suggestion to explore the barn, you knew how it would entice his sense of curiosity. Your peasant blouse flirting a naked shoulder, tiny waist enhanced by full skirt, and bare, tanned legs flashing in the cool of the barn cause another tremor in his penis. The cows' udders have made a photograph on his brain.

Alone, not a soul around, his healthy body pleading for sexual release, you no longer have to be concerned about "making" the Sagittarius male. He's now on the make for you.

Pleasant mown-hay odors and earthy smells of stored oats and barley permeate the air. Six stalls bare of horses, long unused for housing farm animals. Shafts of sunlight, shooting through the high loft windows, making beams of yellow color, enhance the quiet of the barn. The Sagittarian's romantic nature is taking in the sight, fully satisfied that this moment is of special note.

In the far corner of the barn, a pitchfork stands against a stall. He industriously pitches the straw around, taking a great abundance from bales stacked nearby. He prepares a hastily arranged but perfect king-sized, hay-mattressed stall in which to lie.

Merrily you leap on the straw like a child free on summer's vacation. You land in the hay, skirt over your face, laughing with joyful abandon. More sedately your Sagittarian drinks in the picture of your tanned legs apart, arms outspread, hair disheveled, lying on the straw. Like a large, wanton rag doll, totally relaxed.

The elastic in the leg of your panties traces above the tan, exposing a line of white where bathing suit ended, and downy brown hair peeps out, curling on the lacy trim. Quicker now, he rushes to the tantalizing sight, immersing himself in the fragrant hay a hairbreadth away from the curly tendril peeking through the bikini underthing.

His nostrils fill with scents of sun and rain, perfume and

pussy. So compelling, he inadvertently rips the panties in his haste to remove them, exposing a moist and patient kitten, mewing to be petted.

Coitus

Practically overcome by need, your pussy becomes alive, moving in around and grinding motion, hips lifted to meet his inquiring fingers. Watching with absorption while unzipping and forcing his shorts down, he greets your now impatient fuzzy pussy, moving his hand in frantic effort to keep up with the energetic movements of your hips.

You know the Sagittarian needs constant action and change, so deliberately you remove the wet and jerking fingers from within and somersault over and on him. Then, like a playful cat, you straddle his waist, and as you rise to a sitting position, one grapefruit-sized, pink-tipped breast escapes from your blouse. His eye for the unusual makes for a passionate dive to get at that strawberry nipple.

Tenderness gone now and stallion ready, he lifts you with strength he didn't know he had and places you firmly on his penis, pulling off the blouse with his other hand to expose your other luscious fruit. As you press down on his penis, you both sink deep in the hay, locked in each other's arms, totally involved with one another's lusty movements.

At the well again, he pumps and pumps and pumps away. Bringing a refreshing stream of juice on his hard cock. Then quiet, with just the sounds of insects playing their own tunes in accompaniment to his erratic breathing.

Surprise him now. He thinks it's done; not so. Using his handkerchief, remove the creamy residue of your lovemaking. His diminished penis has slipped from its mark, hanging its head, wanting more but uninformed as to your next approach.

Removing your skirt, which is all that's left, you struggle out of and across the hay to the barn floor, headed for the ladder leading to the loft above. A wood nymph with straw in your hair, enticing the gallant Sagittarian to follow.

Games are for him. His sunny disposition is optimistic now that there's more to come. Climb up five steps, then lift one foot onto the sixth rung. He arrives beneath and follows, but with his tongue. He can't resist a sight like that. Athena on her ladder to the kingdom of the gods. You allow him a bit of tongue play, and then scamper to the loft. He dashes up the ladder after you and takes charge of the situation.

"Stand there, woman," and in a snap you do, playing the scene with the born instinct of an actress. He makes a switch of hay, grabbing it tightly at one end, fanning out the other, and proceeds to strike you, simulating a violent attack, in reality just tickling your nakedness as he swishes the blows boldly across your body. As you watch him strike, you see his penis rise. He drops the switch, clutches his penis, and attacks vehemently. Leaning hard against you, he pries into your deepest secrets. Clutching you to him, he thrusts into your wet, hot vagina. It seems to go on and on until you both come together in a final burst.

Post-coitus

Long ago the sun descended and the moon rose. The animal sounds of cows, horses, and dogs are gone. The night is still.

The shafts of sunlight have turned now to silver beams filling the barn with bright light as you hunt for blouse and panties, he for shirt and shorts.

All the while joking, the Sagittarian male has had the time of his life. All was fun and gay and happy. No heavy mad love scenes with tears and pleading.

You can be sure there's more to come. After all, there are other barns, and stables, and haystacks, and . . .

The Sagittarius Woman

Recognition

The Sagittarius woman is usually tall and slender, with a graceful, willowy look. This look predominates until she starts walking. Then, after starting out like a queen, she might stumble two seconds later on a small stone or crack in the sidewalk. With no obstacles around for her to trip over, she can create a stunning impression.

However, she does have an easy, breezy manner, an extremely friendly way about her, and a sunny disposition. She's a gal who bounces back from hurts, depressions, and disappointments.

Her shoulders are well-proportioned, with firm muscles, and she holds up extremely well over the years. Her shoulders are often slightly sloped, the hips tucked under and placed forward. This natural body structure and ability to strike unusual poses makes many Sagittarius women tops in the modeling field.

Her face is usually striking and exotic. Her features may be slightly irregular, but they seem to add rather than detract from her unique beauty.

She'll wear her usually long hair close in around her face, to frame and highlight her features. She's bright and sharp, outspoken, and at times a bit too honest in her opinions. She's a lady of motion, action, and excitement.

The Sagittarius woman is likely to have wavy hair, preferring to comb it back in a warm, soft, casual look, with tendrils or bangs on her forehead. You'll very seldom see her with short-cropped hair, because she likes to let those tresses flow in the breeze. She can be a blond, brunette, or redhead, but quite often her hair color has been tinted to her own particular preference. Her natural color tends to light brown, as do her eyebrows.

Her mouth is a bow, representative of her archer Sagittarian sign, and is very, very beautiful. She can smile exquisitely and is extremely careful about those lovely front teeth.

Her hands are extremely artistic, not long and slender in the accepted aesthetic sense, but fine-boned, capable, and strong. You feel you can put your life in this lady's hands. They're not lazy and languid, either.

She's excellent at makeup, utilizing the minimum to achieve the maximum. She's an optimistic sort and shows it in her cheerful countenance. The face always keeps shining, even though she may be disguising hurt or anger; the latter is a state that doesn't come easily to her.

The Sagittarian woman has individuality—sometimes ignoring fashion to do her own thing, to find a niche somewhere between a plain look and an overly artificial one.

She likes bright, light colors in her clothes. Somber shades affect her badly, and she's a campaigner for combined comfort and style. Comfort is uppermost. In the evening she could wear a gown with a simple cut that allows freedom of movement, not usually tight or slinky. Halter necklines show off her lovely, creamy shoulders. If she's in a kooky mood, she'll likely don an enormous picture hat or even an Australian bush job, to lend affirmation to a knack for always looking striking, for suggesting the out-of-doors, the free and unfettered way of life.

Accessories are not terribly important to this gal. Her jewelry, when she decides to wear it, will be large, chunky, and exotic.

Her perfumes are decidedly meaningful, usually light, spicy scents that are quiet, yet challenging, like carnation. She'll shy away from the sweet-smelling bouquets. Perfumes must be brilliant and striking, not mysterious in the accepted sense of that term.

Quixotically, though, she cares little for accessorizing in the cosmetic field. Any commercial soap is a satisfying choice, and any ordinary deodorant, as long as it does the job. Although she's a nut about washing her hair, personal grooming is not a terribly picky subject.

Where to Find Her

This lady loves to walk along a sunny seashore, hair loosened to the breezes. She isn't averse to public beaches, either, and likes the force of waves, allowing them to knock her down for the sheer athletic fun of it. She thrives on water sports and scuba-diving. Look for her near the water or just lying in the sun. Most Sagittarius gals are fine water-skiers.

At the other end of the spectrum, the theater, especially light comedies, are a special delight. It only follows that many Sagittarians are famous in the acting field, and become involved in this chosen career early in life. They're really born actresses. Even when they're feeling low, you won't know it. They are always a wonder to be around, shedding sunlight, never gloom.

The Sagittarian is frank at all costs. This directness is not aimed at hurting anyone, merely utilized as a tool of her absolute honesty. She'll cannily cover this frankness with charm if she feels she's offended anyone.

You'll find her at hospitals doing volunteer work, possibly with drug groups. She has a way of dealing with people that is both affirmative and stern at the same time. She never sits in judgment, offers understanding above all, and really cares about helping people.

Public relations, publicity, and advertising fields are good career choices, plus an ability as a good manager of talents other than her own. There is also an adeptness in the field of producing art shows, exhibitions, and concerts for artists in other cultural and aesthetic fields. Her marvelous taste in furniture and fabrics makes her well-suited for a career in interior design.

As for sports, you'll spot her easily at hockey games and boxing or wrestling matches, watching man pitted against man, strength against strengh. She's quite a gal, this one, very, very involved.

Primary Move

Your best approach to a Sagittarius woman is to appeal to her wonderful appetite. An invitation to dine is usually most acceptable, no matter where you want to take her. She's just as much at home in a gourmet restaurant as in a meadow with a picnic basket or at a barbecue. Even though a lover of unusual and creative sauces, she still wants to taste the meat. Shrimp scampi is just about number one with many Sagittarius women. Although she'll be most pleased with any seafood cuisine, cheese, bread, and wine under a spreading summer tree will make her just as content. Corn is a great fun food for this lady, and she will absolutely swoon over artichokes any way they're prepared.

She likes pumpkin, turnips, and can eat more pasta than most men, doting on macaroni, spaghetti, linguine, and anything else that has the Neapolitan or Sicilian touch. Taste in wine is plain, leaning toward dry white wine and Chianti.

Her real hang-up is dessert. Her slender body bespeaks a good diet, but she's a glutton for anything rich, anything containing generous portions of rum, chocolate, and lots of whipped cream. You'll wonder how she keeps her extraordinary figure, even into late maturity.

This girl will appreciate and acknowledge a "right-on" approach. If she's standing in the sea waiting for a wave to slam into her, walk right up and see if you can match the fascination of that wave. Tell her you've been watching her and that you think she's delicious to see. She'll like the directness, because that quality is one of her trademarks.

She loves animals, naturally gravitating to best-of-breed shows where cats, dogs, or horses are concerned. Especially interesting is the breeding of aristocrats, and her love of anything beautiful definitely includes the animal kingdom. Her interest, however, is largely in shows and the animals themselves, not in the racing scene. You can more often than not get a quick "yes" with an invitation to one of these events.

Flattery isn't really necessary. Say it as it is and she'll accept you for what you are. Hopefully, you can in turn accept her frankness. If you can, you've got it made!

What's on this girl's mind usually comes right out of her beautiful mouth; she'll let you have it, no holds barred! If you'd like to take her out for the evening, don't withhold the facts, whether it's to be a party for six or a private affair for just you two.

Nature really turns this lady on. She's great fun, totally honest, and most important for some men, makes few demands on your freedom.

Pre-coitus

The Sagittarius woman is versatile, open-minded, and adaptable. Her nature is such that a quick change of scene or plan does not interfere with her fluidity of movement. She thrills to the exotic choice of words and experiences extolled in Krafft-Ebing and the Masters and Johnson reports. She is willingly adaptable as long as it involves just you, but bring a third party or more into a romantic situation, and she tightens up like a pilgrim at a witch trial in Salem.

The Sagittarian loves to have sex in a big open field with bright sunlight overhead. For example, you may be driving along the countryside on a back road, admiring the full blossom of the corn fields and ripening wheat. If you chance to catch a glimpse of two dogs, one mounted on the other, she will most likely start squirming in the seat beside you. Nature and its pregnant fruitfulness is a great stimulant to her sexually.

She likes you to handle her like a caveman handles his woman; so be direct; handle her firmly. Don't let her think you're hesitant or unsure of yourself.

You don't have to engage in any mid-Victorian, romanticized, old-fashioned courtship with a Sagittarius woman. She likes to be a pal to men, so don't try to place her on a pedestal. She likes to laugh, so be funny, original, and frank in your sexual conversations with her. Although her sense of humor is excellent, so-called "bathroom" jokes aren't acceptable. Oddly amusing sexual jokes with surprise punch lines are what she likes.

She enjoys talking bluntly about sex, so get her on the subject, and speculate about having sex with her in odd circumstances. Just the talk and thought of unusual places or times for sex will give her a full sense of joy. This is a lusty type of person who reacts favorably to strange tales of erotica.

The Sagittarian likes travel and sports. Keep her free and on the go. Wherever you take her, make sure you're giving her the sense of freedom that is so necessary. Be inventive and unique in your sexual adventures with her, but don't be bizarre. She appreciates and will react favorably to a walk along the ocean's edge just after twilight, wearing a bikini, you in your bathing trunks. Then suggest to her, "Let's walk along with your bikini top off." Not her bottoms, just the bra. The movement of her breasts, dancing up and down, free of encumbrance, while first pacing briskly, then slowing down, and then speeding up again, could lead then and there to the inevitable. She'll luxuriate in the feel of bare breasts moving freely.

Above all, don't corner her; it gives her claustrophobia. No small cozy rooms with just one window and a candle; no closets or bathtubs for her. Don't try the back seat of a car or any cramped place with this woman. Don't even try playing footsies under the table in a social situation, or in all likelihood your Sagittarian will be definitely cool by dessert time. In fact, while at dinner, lean toward her and whisper something mundane in her ear. Say it quietly and huskily, rolling the words with your tongue—"Apple pie or crêpes suzette?"—as if you could taste it. She'll react as if you had her in your arms in a private dining room. If anything works with a Sagittarius woman, it's giving her a choice of two or more of anything, even desserts.

You'll discover that the lady of the bow and arrow is happy, warm-hearted, and optimistic. You can play wonderful sexual games with her. After finding a "deserted" house and investigating by yourself, suggest an adventure and take her to the abandoned estate. Make love to her against the banister of a circular staircase. Plan ahead for a lone visit to make sure there are no broken floorboards and there's no rubbish on the floor. Holding her hand, tiptoe through an investigation of the "haunted house." After snooping through a room or two, pull her to you quickly, as if you heard a noise. "What was that?" She'll cling closer because of the suddenness of the moment. Fright will leave and be replaced by sexual desire. It is the unusual scene, circumstance, and prevailing mood that are enticing.

Since the great outdoors is so intriguing, make love to her again in the nearby woods, lying on a bed of pine needles, listening to the cars go by a few feet away.

The Sagittarius woman is grandiose in sexual matters. She needs space. So if you prefer a hotel, make sure the suite is lavish and the bed king-sized.

Coitus

The Sagittarius woman has to be shown you are a man. Remember, she likes you to handle her caveman style, so lying there on your bed of pine needles and grass, handle her firmly and directly. Take hold of your penis and murmur,

The Lovers' Guide to Sensuous Astrology 143

"This is yours, all yours. It's big for you. Show me what you'll do with your hips when I let you have it." That ache begins, and she'll move with a motion so swift that nothing more than your erotic conversation and her sensuous movements may bring on an orgasm.

Don't spend a great deal of time on delicate foreplay before coitus with this woman. If the entrance to her vagina is wet, she's ready. If you've got a big penis, so much the better for you. She'll want it all! In any event, be sure you've got lots of stamina and virile strength. There on the ground, make the first meeting of direct intercourse quickly.

If you see her interest waning, you must manufacture excitement without losing your own control. It's wise to let her wear herself out after her first climax. Withdraw before you ejaculate, think about baseball or whatever works for you. That should turn you off, but keep her desire at a high pitch by asking her to assume some suggestive positions. Stay away from her while being the director. Tell her she's on stage, the star, and you're producing the show. Ask her to stand facing the tree a few feet away from her, rear end toward you. Now tell her to spread her legs apart and place her hands against the tree. Say, "Reach for me, reach for my penis. I'll come toward you, but you try to snatch my penis, try to insert it." This gets her moving in a backward-and-forward motion, stretching all her muscles, tiring her to a degree, but this is important with the Sagittarian. She likes to be handled especially rough during sexual intercourse. Wrestle her, pin her down, engage her in action. Grab her hips, insert your penis, almost rape her. She likes to feel your manliness, your maleness, your virile sexual power over her. She likes the basic reality of sex, so be sure you give it to her.

You can interrupt coitus again by playing an imaginative game. This will help you to contain your own ardor and will fully satisfy her. Using a clean handkerchief or her own panties or hose, gently—and it must be gently—blindfold her. Use your thumb while she's lying back, totally inserted in her vagina. As she moves in ecstasy, and if you're up to it, manufacture a tale of kidnap and forceful seduction. With her eyes blindfolded and the action of your thumb then fingers, it won't be but a moment or two before you're making love to this woman again. Tell her about it, that it's you now, not your fingers, and this will excite her all the more. You can use some four-letter words with her during the heat of sex.

Tell her that you just want to knead her hips, fondle

those breasts, massage that round bottom of hers. That you want to get your prick in her cunt and fuck her. Be blunt, direct. Describe whatever you're doing as you're doing it. Ask her if she likes your hands on her nipples. Tell her that her clitoris is pulsating like your penis. That it's hard, and you want to feel it with your tongue. Deftly cup the clitoris by rolling your tongue around it; keep your tongue and mouth away from her vagina. Her sensitivity will be so high-pitched that once again you've established your maleness and she has climaxed. Continue telling her how her vulva is soft and that you are going to wrap yourself up within her being. She's not shy, so you can speak to her directly. If you want her to take your penis in her mouth and suck it, tell her that you're removing your penis from within her and that you are finding your way over her downy, soft mound of venus, past her breasts, then into her sucking mouth. Tell her to stroke up and down the shaft with her tongue. Instruct her to lap around the head of your penis, teething it lightly. You can tell her to move her mouth to the left testicle and devour it carefully and completely, then to the right testicle. When she's finished tasting and savoring your manhood, arrange your body so that you're kneeling between her legs. Now tell her to open her legs wide and bend them at the knees. Tell her all this protectively in order to give her pleasure. Be the kind but forceful male. Quickly insert your penis, and just when she's ready to have an orgasm again, let yourself go. Now's the time, and it's perfection. By conversation, make her ask for more, and then come back stronger than ever. You can be rough and conversational with the Sagittarius woman, but remember, always be the total *male*.

Post-coitus

When it's over, the Sagittarian will be dreamy. In the great outdoors, she'll be looking at the moon, feeling part of the world, and equating herself with the brightest star in the heavens. Now is the time to be quiet with her. Do not talk to her, and do not touch her. Leave her totally alone. Stay away from her body and let her commune with nature and the life force. Let her be the one to decide to dress, stand up, or move. Follow her lead after lovemaking. Be there, but don't intrude on her body or her thoughts. Commune with her by putting a field flower in her hand. You'll find that her humor is excellent at this point. You're a lucky man, and if you desire to continue the relationship, don't hesitate to tell her so when she stirs to dress.

The Sagittarian loves to hear how much you enjoyed the expression of passion and will drink up any detailed stories you tell her about it being one of the most fantastic times, sexually, in your life.

You'll find that as you drive her home she'll question you specifically, like, "How did you feel when you blindfolded me? Was it exciting?" Then she'll ask, "When I backed into your penis, was it better than just lying on the ground?" She's a glutton for sex talk, so do it. Conversation can be very stimulating to you, too. Who knows, as you're driving by some old covered bridge on the way home, you might ask her if she'd like to stop and ... she might say yes!

CAPRICORN
(December 22–January 20)

The Capricorn Man

Recognition

The Capricorn man is really the personification of business in its total essence, including all the dog-eat-dog opportunism, hard work, planning, scheming, conning, success, and failure. He's completely wrapped up in work, work, work, in any sort of business, always looking for new ways to achieve success. If it comes fast, he's surprised. Used to plodding and perseverance, he'll settle in for the stay, prepared for any eventuality.

He dislikes the physical sort of battle, but handles verbal fencing well. Capricorn is usually medium height and wiry, with high cheekbones and a particularly prominent brow. His head is quite often larger than expected for his frame. He gives an impression of intense seriousness. His nose is generally aquiline, and well-suited for a face such as his. His lips are sometimes thin and small, but with a devastating smile that he doesn't use often enough.

Capricorn men carry with them an air of distinction about their appearance. An intent, purposeful look, one that convinces others of their trustworthiness and dependability.

He has an extremely bright and alert expression that clearly says that he's ever seeking opportunities and advancement in business.

He may seem cold, this Capricornian, but it's just a veneer.

He's actually searching for warmth and admiration from others. Once he has found that certain someone he's been seeking and has fallen in love, her devotion and attention are as essential as food to him.

Capricorn, even after his intense search, finds it difficult to express his feelings in words, those little endearments used to keep a woman happy.

A conversation overheard at the wedding reception of a Capricorn and his bride goes like this. He says, "Why are you so sad, it's your wedding day. You're not sick, are you?"

She says, "No, it's just that you never tell me you love me, do you?"

He says matter-of-factly, "My dear, if I didn't love you, I wouldn't be here today!" and if she loves him, she has to settle for that endearing statement. And you can be sure if they are together for fifty years, she'll still be asking the same question and he'll still be giving the same answer.

Promiscuity is not his way when he finds the woman who is his fulfillment. He's enormously faithful and very involved, even if he doesn't spend much time with his loved one. His love is deep and long-lasting; he is always giving and understanding, except with words of love and romantic phrases.

The Capricorn goat is also self-willed to a point of distraction, strong in his views, hard to change, dynamically ambitious, as well as pensive and reserved. You can learn to read the signs—a twitching of the fingers, or a nervous rocking of a crossed leg. He's self-reliant to the point of seeming not to need you, but he *does!*

Many Capricornians are kind in a somewhat aloof way, understanding in a professional way, and are always ready to offer a helping hand in an impersonal way. But don't underestimate them for these fine human qualities. Don't analyze it as a sign of weakness, for whatever business they're in, they can be dangerous adversaries. The Capricorn male's surface is cold and calculating, like an IBM computer. They waste not, but they want and need money to buy what's required to serve whatever their purpose may be. Governed by the planet Saturn, their saturnine personality sometimes sags easily into depression. Just your presence and consideration (without too much talk but lots of warmth) can pull him right out of his gloom. He's cunning, and uses other's weaknesses to make himself stronger. If not self-employed, at his work he'll do anything he's told by those in command, until he becomes indispensable; then he easily moves in and takes over!

It seems the Capricorn man can exist happily even when totally and completely alone, not sharing his life with a woman. No man is an island, they say, but he could very well be one. He might not care for that existence, but is usually hesitant in settling for second best. He'd rather take his chances, be lonely now and then, than share his life with someone who is not truly compatible.

His wardrobe is conventional and conservative down to his white underwear. His clothes range from dark brown to black. The proverbial gray flannel suit is his favorite. Capricorn might feel "wild" in a conservative cocoa suit with a bright orange tie. He'll probably wear the tie once, then put it away, saving it along with lots of other items he wouldn't wear. Somehow the "goat" cannot bring himself to throw things out that are of no use to him. Rather, he stores them in bureau drawers, on top shelves in closets, and in boxes under his bed. His nature is not one of procrastination, but when it comes to throwing out old clothes, "I'll do it tomorrow . . ." and tomorrow never comes.

Then he'll latch on to wearing a handkerchief folded a special way in his suit-coat pocket. Even though that style became extinct in the 1930's, he'll adopt it and fold a new one each day and tuck it in his pocket just so.

You could say he has a fetishistic nature, and it goes along with his insatiable search for just the right woman.

It might be the size of her feet that captures him, her tiny waist, or long, exquisitely manicured fingernails.

It could be the perfume she uses, or her smile. Maybe the curve of her calf or the way her buttocks sway when she walks. Who knows with the Capricorn—only him! But once he's convinced she's the one, just like the goat, he'll climb precipitous rocky crags to get her, undaunted in his quest.

Where to Find Him

Capricorn men make excellent computer programmers because they're cautious and exact. The millions of details in setting up a new system can keep them occupied hour after hour, giving little or no thought to time of day. These attributes also assist them in being fine accountants and bookkeepers as well, able to make order and form out of chaos. A Capricorn man can step into a bankrupt business, and by walking through the offices or factory, just by casting a few knowing glances, can spot the major causes of trouble. This facility is so well-developed that many factories and corporations employ lists of Capricorns. His one stroll around the premises enables him to show the owners how the business could be saved at little cost or rearrangement and utilization of personnel. He's thoroughly basic and good at taking over *after* others' initial creativity and imagination are applied. He easily sets in motion the systems, forms, and procedures required.

The demands made by any branch of the armed services and the recognition of accomplishment established by the conferring of increased rank according to performance could encourage the Capricorn male to become a career military officer. He's basically a stern disciplinarian, and if not in administrative services, he's probably the top sergeant thousands of veterans have cursed throughout their military sojourns.

Many Capricornians manage foundations that invest other people's money for profit to be used for philanthropic purposes. Their integrity and honesty serves well here.

Is pleasure actually unknown to this severe, calculating, serious, business-oriented male? That's a very difficult question to answer. A Capricornian's avocation, hobby, or pleasure is not run-of-the-mill. He could enjoy community-project involvement, not promulgating it, but setting it in motion and running it. He particularly enjoys reading nonfiction, war novels, adventure stories, and biographies. Swimming isn't too much effort, so he'll do it, and if he has any flair at all for strenuous activity, he'll take to horseback riding. He's more the sports observer than the participant. He much prefers watching a game at home on TV to being in the stadium crowd.

Primary Move

Since the pleasure aspect of approach to the Capricorn man is limited, you must think along those lines of his interest that could include you. He's such an organizer, and so serious, your best move for immediate acceptance is an impersonal approach. Knock on his door or intentionally bump into him on the street. Tell him, for instance, that you feel very strongly about the lack of information in your area about where working mothers can take their children for day care. Or you could use any other similar excuses. How you can help unwed mothers or introduce a breakfast program for the elderly. Any sort of community gambit is all right. Be prepared, though, to follow through, once he prepares a program. Like the goat, he'll tenaciously stick to your progress reports until he's satisfied you're really on your way with it.

Add that you're intersted in starting a committee but don't know how to go about carrying out your ideas. This is the kind of project he can take in hand, and he'll very probably bite. The wheels of organization will start to spin speedily through his coordinated brain. Ask him to stop by your place and bring along his plan and any information that may be helpful. Tell him you're great with ideas, but helpless at coordinating projects like this, and you'll be pushing in the right direction. He'll like this, and it's a good way to get him to warm up to you.

After a discussion, he's hungry, so feed him earthly food on the coffee table or on a TV table. If you're in a sweater and blue jeans, look natural but never sloppy.

As to food, he'll consume anything if it's well-prepared. His favorites are the "dark" foods—black bread, sautéed mushrooms, pickled beets, chopped liver. Steaks and chops are preferred to complicated or casserole dishes, and he likes them served rare.

Soups are a special favorite, hot or cold. Both male and female Capricornians are born with a perpetual thirst, and this could grow into a problem. If their self-control or love life is threatened, then alcohol could become a terrifying reality. Aside from liquor, any liquid is all right, be it tea, soda pop, or just plain water. Feed him garlic, pepper, broccoli, and lots of really tasty things like artichokes and spareribs.

While having a snack, steer the conversation to personal issues, more about yourself than him. Make sure he knows you're a one-man woman and don't stand in judgment of others. Kiss him warmly, impulsively, on the cheek. If there's no reaction, say it was just for "thanks." He'll thaw then, mind you, so be patient. He reacts to temperature, and if it's cold outside and it's close to bedtime ... well, you can never really predict what he'll think or do next.

If you've really observed your subject, you've probably noted that he latches on to specific "things." For example, the clothes syndrome and his inability to dispose of them. Or his penchant for a specific "thing" about a female—that'll really get him. Keep your fingers crossed and your lips smiling.

Who knows, maybe it's the way your sweater defines your breasts that fascinates him.

Pre-coitus

Saturn rules the man. The serious, energetic, down-to-earth personality of our saturnine Capricorn male.

He's like a ball of twine knotted together on one huge roll. If undone, the string is seemingly endless—miles and miles of man. Always there, always dependable. In a crisis, someone to call upon for help. In need, a man who always comes through. And in love, a huge question mark, but ordinarily a guaranteed fine performance.

It's important for him to display his strength and knowhow, to put his best foot forward for you as well as for the world. This is an important function for his well-being. He cares what others think and carries himself with dignity but no affectation. Rather than display a temper, he'll let you know he's displeased by his icy-cold attitude. It's impossible to reach him then. This escape is his way out when angry or annoyed if you joke with him and he's the goat! His nature neither permits him to love easily nor to laugh easily at himself. In fact, perhaps his greatest fault is that his sense of humor is limited. This lack is overcome by his inner strength and determined ability to bore his way through all problematical situations. Capricorn is a capable and tenacious man who will take on the world to ram his way through to achieving his goals.

Right now, though, he's your goal, and if he's mentioned your lovely full lower lip more than once, that's it! You've found that particular quality about yourself that so attracts him. Use your mouth now to gain your ultimate end. After straightening up the living room and piling the dishes in the kitchen sink, excuse yourself.

Using a lipstick brush, carefully repair your lipstick, using a natural lip tone. Use more than you usually do, because the aim is to employ his own tactics, using his weakness and your mouth to achieve your own end.

Return to him smiling. Taking his hands upturned in yours, kiss each palm, leaving an imprint of your lips there.

Then lean toward his mouth, kissing him squarely on the lips, parting yours so he can feel your teeth against his. He may be less prone to passion than some of the other signs of the zodiac, but aware of your purpose, he'll return the kiss.

And in the same way he goes about concluding a business deal, he'll methodically return your kiss, trying different positions of the mouth, experimenting with his tongue and teeth, most anxious to please you.

By the time he's through, your mouth will feel it's been whirled through an eggbeater. He doesn't stop at anything until the job's done.

Once you've made the first move, turn the lead over to him. Remember, top sergeants love putting rookies through their paces. Like the perfectionist he is, he wants to see in the light of day what he's getting. There's every possibility he'll ask you to remove your clothes, standing there in front of him, then to walk up and back, showing off your good points like a captured enemy princess at the slave market.

Use this moment to your own advantage. Instead of clumsily or quickly hopping out of your things, remove each piece of clothing with an elegance and sensuousness that could melt an iceberg.

Stand with your back to him, legs apart, and lift your sweater slowly up, moving your body ever so slightly from side to side as it glides over your breasts. Turn around then, facing him, and let him get the full effect as you pull the sweater over your head.

His eyes will tell you that you know what you're doing, and doing it well.

Bring a dining-room chair into the room, placing it directly in front of him; sit on it with your legs apart. Bend over voluptuously to remove each shoe, putting them neatly as a pair under your chair. Then suck in your stomach, all the while smiling, and reach with both hands behind your back to unsnap your bra. Holding your arm under your breasts, with the other hand slowly pull each strap from your shoulders. Pull the bra away, exposing each mound, tipped with an extended nipple. Look down at your breasts, rubbing them in delight because they're free from restriction.

Watch how, as you do this, Capricorn's penis is coming to attention. It's quite evident all's going well.

Take a break from disrobing, and still on your knees, go to him, breasts swaying seductively. Unzip his fly and pull his erect penis from between his legs into full view. Then stand, step back, and start to unzip your jeans, lasciviously wiggling your hips as you pull both slacks and panties down over your hips; then let them drop to the floor.

Walk around him like a showgirl, proud of your nude

body, and don't be surprised if he asks you to sit on the floor and then crawls in front of you. Although still dressed, his magnificent pole continues poking into your thigh. Grab it and rub it. Trace your thumb and index finger over the head. Then let your palm run down its full length, picking up the rhythm as you move your hand up and down. Faster, faster, until he's breathing heavily; then stop, smile again, bend down, and suck his rearing stud.

His faculty for fingering you will enchant you. He has a way of taking command that's positively stimulating. Gently forcing you down on the rug, he'll remain between your legs, watching each squirm of your hips as he inserts his fingers. Keeping up a steady rhythm, he'll manipulate your clitoris, energetically massaging the entire vulva area until you've felt orgasm.

Meanwhile, his penis is erect and as much at attention as when you started. He'll remove his trousers and other clothing now, everything in its place, and will tweak and pluck each urgent nipple.

All this foreplay is of great meaning with Capricorn. Once he's chosen to share his body, he must satisfy you completely, or it's not a task well done—and that's forbidden in his book.

Just as your lips were used until they tingled, so will your vulva feel you've honeymooned a week, and still no coitus. He's ready now to enter, sensing he's accomplished his present purpose.

Coitus

Rambling through your mental storehouse of Capricorn data, if you've been a good student, you'll remember he takes over once a situation has been initiated by others. So let him be the guide to your moment of meaning. The pulsing vagina is twofold. Physical from the recent stimulation of all your sensual parts, also pulsing for the entrance of his penis. You picture it as a battering ram breaking down a prison wall to free all the pent-up desire you've built for this Capricorn.

Lifting you bodily from the floor, his wiry strength is evident now. He'll carry you into your bedroom and place you in perfect position on the bed, head on a pillow and body relaxed comfortably on the sheet.

Lying beside you, he'll encompass you in his arms, pressing your breasts tightly against his chest and his penis between your thighs. Holding you like this, he'll start a rocking motion with his hips, forcing yours to move in cohesively close action with his.

Searching your mouth with his tongue, he'll dart it in and out and at the same time will reposition your hips so he can enter. As the first thrust comes, he doesn't lose a beat in his rhythmic movement, only now he's holding you tighter and his rocklike penis is pushing higher and harder within as his mouth sucks on your tongue and lips. One long gigantic kiss until your mind becomes a black cloud and your body one long drum roll interrupted only when he ejaculates.

It's unlikely there'll be a repeat performance then and there. Upon examination, you'll probably find your inner thighs black and blue, your labia swollen, your vagina deliciously sore, and your mouth devastated beyond belief. The only antidote to Capricorn lovemaking, to become whole again, is sleep.

Post-coitus

Business finished, goal achieved, he'll pat you on the fanny, order you to sleep, roll over and hit dreamland himself. Although you'd like to lie awake awhile to relive some of those wild feelings, you're physically exhausted and will nod off before you hear him snoring in restful sleep.

The moment of awakening the next morning can be cruel. You'll discover muscles you didn't know you had in your back, arms, and legs. The aches will renew the entire night before, and instead of pain, you'll feel the thrill of really having been loved.

If you can take a long, hot tub bath, filled with epsom salt, to relieve those sore spots before he awakes, it'll be just grand. You'd walk like a wrestler that's out of condition, and Capricorn mustn't see that.

Luxuriate awhile after filling the tub with a few drops of your favorite bath oil. Take a cold shower afterward, and upon your return to the bed to cuddle, you'll find him patiently waiting for the john, a towel he took from your linen closet in hand. With not a word, just a peck on the cheek, he goes to perform his morning ablutions.

Of course, you know now you're wholly committed! There are no ifs, ands, or buts. When he returns to the bedroom to dress and says, "I'll be here at eight this evening," just smile.

You've got what you wanted, and gametime is over. This is the real thing.

The Capricorn Woman

Recognition

This lady has to feel that the entire world is looking at her through rose-colored glasses. What's more, this public she's so bent on impressing has got to appreciate what they see. Ms. Capricorn simply has to feel that only good things are being said about her, and she suffers terribly if it's the reverse. It's prosperity all the way with the Capricorn woman.

Married or single, she's the power behind her husband or boyfriend, strong, determined, possessing great talent for organization and for guiding the man in the right direction. If there's no man in her life, she becomes the object of her own tenacity, and this generally petite woman is a powerhouse at pushing herself toward her goals.

Her face is generally long and thin, with high cheekbones, an ideal model for Modigliani, and she is immediately identifiable by her pronounced temples, prominent brow, and diminutive height. She has a small, determined mouth and thin lips. She doesn't talk verbosely, but exudes charm through her divine, illuminating smile. As a hostess, she more often than not has business in the back of her mind and is out to make an impression.

The Capricorn woman's hair is finely textured, usually brunette to black, and the hair styles she affects are understated, as is her clothing. Her diminutive stature and slender face do not call for complicated coiffures. She is the kind of woman who will wear a variety of wigs. As the years pass, she seems to get younger-looking and more beautiful. There's generally no weight problem here, because her energy burns up calories fast. Her most serious problem is sinking too frequently into depressions, but as she grows older and keeps her mind and her body occupied, this tendency decreases.

Her legs are slim, and her bust is usually not overlarge. For the man who delights in the boyish, teen-age figure, the Capricorn woman is perfection.

Some may feel that as a personality she's an opportunist, and this is partly true. She's straightforward about it, never going about her goal-gaining in a surreptitious fashion. She'll use people around her, but she's not secretive, and lets them know where it's at and what she's about. This is a mandatory part of her performance, a part of her character that must be exhibited. She's a dynamo at her chosen work, reserved in her demeanor, constricted in exuding warmth, inhibited in female friendships, uptight if she doesn't get her way, and completely charming. Capricorn is truly a complex personality.

A computer-minded soul who registers every incident and files away the card, the Capricorn girl seems to be constantly clearing obstacles in her path. It seems as if from birth she never forgets, and she'll find a way, even years later, to repay a good deed or a kindness. She's very sensitive, particularly in family areas, and just can't take it if you criticize her relatives. She feels that they should be just as ultraperfect in your eyes as they obviously are in hers.

Although her appearance sometimes suggests a light frost has settled in, it's just a front, really. She's constantly afraid of being hurt, and withdraws quickly. Her principles for justice to all are high, and unless committed to a man, her morals are too. Promiscuity in sex is not an overt preoccupation with the Capricorn lady. She's self-willed and a good listener, concentrating on the talker and holding secrets tight. But she's conniving, too, and if she feels someone can help her improve herself or advance her position, she's not hesitant about using them and telling them so. Even romantically, she'll use someone, but once infatuated and compelled, she gets down to brass tacks quickly, a very earthy, passionate sort, methodical and determined to achieve happiness, more for her lover than for herself.

As to fashion, she's understated as opposed to flashy, displaying good breeding through choice of grays, blacks, and browns in dark hues, utilizing quiet mixtures of color. She's either indifferent to style or a seeker of total perfection. She'll be miserable if her stockings don't match. Jewelry is not important to her. Her almost luminescent self provides an inner spark that requires no fashion additives.

The Capricorn female has peculiar tastes in food, liking traditional preparation and ordinary dishes. Dining is for conversation and companionship to this lady. She shines as a hostess with the feeling she doesn't have to prove anything to anyone. She'll prefer earthy foods, the sort pulled from the ground—mushrooms, potatoes, carrots—and favors the sharpness of vinaigrette or sour pickles and horseradish mustard. Walnuts and pistachios take the place of candy for her. She's sensitive to temperatures in both food and living. If she lives in the north, she enjoys the cold weather. Down south, she'll have the air-conditioner going full tilt.

Of all the signs, she's most addicted to cold soups—cold borsch with spinach or beets, vichyssoise and jellied madrilene—and when it comes to liquids, she'll flip over a cool glass of water just as enthusiastically as she will over a smooth Scotch. She's quite a woman, with a seemingly masculine drive in business, but very feminine and fragile-looking. The Capricorn female is generally physically strong, although it would appear she'd blow away like a feather in a breeze.

Where to Find Her

Give this girl some mixed-up situation where she can display her talents for overcoming obstacles, and she's very happy. Tiny, but tough enough to keep her head above water, the Capricorn woman's fantastic organizational ability, her tenacity in handling complex matters, and her ability to strive for and follow through to her goals see her through no matter how inundating the flood. She'll always forge ahead, allowing nothing to stand in her way. This indefatigable energy she possesses enables her to pitch in, sort out tangles, and relish changes that may occur during her attack on a difficult project. She'd be great in the stock market, where there's constant change, and has a good ear for record production. The forming of social or political groups is her forte. Once started and moving, she'll retire to the background but always be the ever-present "power." If she's part of a social club, rest assured she'll be working on the philanthropic committee. She exudes authority and has got to be the top banana. If she's not, she'll surely be the top assistant to the top man. She'd be an exceptionally good stage manager, because she handles people and details beautifully, taking over and seeing things through to the finish.

Hobbies are just not her thing, and artistically her interest could be in knitting, crocheting, or needlework. Something just to keep her hands busy. Hooking rugs is a marvelous pastime for Capricorn. Business is her real fun, her activity, her achievement, and you'll find her involved in solving Chinese puzzles, pulling magic rings apart, or trying to open magician's boxes. Total relaxation is not necessary to her, but momentary refreshment can be found in saunas and steam baths, ironic in such a skinny dame, when it's the fatties who need this. The hot-cold treatment really pleases her, this usually utterly fascinating Capricorn gal.

Primary Move

Since this lady is so strong on family ties, it would be advisable to invite the tribe—mother, father, sister, and brother, and even their mates—to a dinner party. Make sure as the evening progresses that you express appreciation of their attributes.

If so, you've accomplished feat number one. Project number two comes next. With her guard now down a bit, pursue the issue and suggest that the younger members of the family join you for a visit to the "in" place in town, a discotheque or a nightclub. You're right on the button there. The Capricorn girl likes to be seen in all the "right" places.

The third move is to suggest a highball with the folks, in a dimly lit, glamorous spot with haunting music. But be sure you still keep the conversation directed at the family, who may be tiring and ready to depart. While they're leaving, whisper to her that you'd like to see her apartment. Three strikes and she's already out, and your foot's on third base, stealing for home.

Don't be surprised if your Capricorn miss suggests you take her relatives home, dropping her off at her apartment. It'll give her a little time to "straighten up" the place for your return.

Perfect gentleman that you are, you'll concur.

Pre-coitus

This scene takes place before your return.

Daintily attired in four-inch black satin platform mules, she stalks swiftly across the room.

She walks from her full-length mirror in the bedroom to the bathroom mirror, after having struck a pose like a model in porno magazines. There she smiles at herself in satisfaction of how well she looked standing with her legs apart, hands on her hips, both breasts exposed, staring back at her from the glass with their little brown eyes.

Examining her teeth, she smiles languorously. Her image looks back with drooping eyelids, a false eyelash separating itself from the right corner of her right eye. Frantically, out comes the adhesive ... dab ... dab. There, it's set. Smiles again, delighted with the mirrored reflection. Back to the living room now, her gait is enlivened by sounds of "This Could Be the Start of Something Big," jerkily rendered. Ignoring the refrain, she keeps repeating the title, "This Could Be the Start of Something Big."

The darling, diminutive Capricorn moving and singing. A vision in a sheer black negligee, her finely proportioned figure shadowy-silhouetted through the gossamer fabric, exquisite and inviting admiration.

Mister, you've missed this little prelude. But don't be concerned. First, you've got the goods or you wouldn't be coming back to her apartment in the first place. Second, you're in the running for an executive position with your company. Capricorn lady knows this, and her cap was pointed in your direction long before your primary move ever got rolling.

Just remember, her aggressiveness is decoyed by femininity. You'll have no trouble making a score.

The clock in the steeple across the square from the swanky apartment building she lives in strikes one A.M. as you tap the brass knocker on her door. The knocker is representative of the zodiac sign, the ram's horns tapping against a miniature globe. Just like our Capricorn mistress. Knocking her head against the world to win. Opening the door with a flourish, she gestures you in. She closes the door and walks with a light tread, brushing by you just beyond your touch. She gives you an opportunity to really see her. Capricorn is at her most mysterious loveliness. She lures you to her by exposing an ivory-tinged thigh as she sits in a gold velvet chaise in her living room. You'll respond, because she's a delectable dish. A cherry-nectar-filled chocolate candy ready to chew. As you approach her, she gracefully ducks your reaching arms and heads for the balcony. There she beckons with an inviting finger that is tipped by a long, exquisitely manicured, red-painted nail. He who hesitates is lost, but you can't help but stare at her in amazement. You wonder how this very businesslike lady who runs her department like a Simon Legree and handles her people like a tough marine sergeant can also be so utterly gorgeous, glamorous, and feminine.

She an assistant to an officer of your company and has a reputation of being totally cold and uninterested in any affairs with the younger men in the firm. Who's to question? Certainly not you! You want her, made your first move, and here she is practically doing a sexual somersault to entice you.

Fully dressed, you're chilly out there on the sixteenth-floor terrace and wondering how her goose bumps must be. Perfect gentleman, you'll embrace her. Even Capricorn can't resist. Glamour is one thing but it's cold.

Not for long. As you wrap your arms around her from the back, you can feel her nipples standing out like two bullets, holding out the delicate fiber of her gown. The nipples are at least a quarter of an inch long and a half-inch in diameter. The most inactive penis would stiffen seeing this, and so he does.

She feels your hardness through the filmy gown tucking her between her cheeks. Ever ready to encourage you, she bends a bit, pushing her bottom more firmly into your hard-on. What do you do with a horny lady like this? Let her ram you. By this time her goose bumps have given birth to goslings, and her shivering is a combination of cold and desire. Take over now and suggest the warmth of her living room. She'll be the obedient siren as she swishes her way back into the apartment. Meanwhile, you've got an enormous hard-on making a considerable bulge in your pants. She doesn't miss a trick. Capricorn stops short, reaching around you to close the sliding terrace door. As she does so, her elegant hand grabs for your erection. She swiftly opens the zipper, and your penis is on view in its most vivid state. You reach to unsnap the waist of your trousers. She shakes her head. "Not yet!"

She now takes you by the hand to the linen closet next to her bedroom and slides out a black box from under a stack of fluffy towels. Handing it to you, she removes the lid, revealing a duplicate penis, much like yours, only larger. A diagram isn't required. You place her on the floor in the narrow vestibule. Tight quarters, but who cares? Still dressed, your engorged organ is being constantly ogled by her admiring eyes. She's magnetized by its size and persistence. You're amazed by your own control. Goose bumps again, this time yours, as you kneel beside her. In tight quarters you slide the dildo into her vagina. Not a sound from her as it invades her privacy. You're breathing hard now. Higher it goes, and unless you hold on tightly, the suction almost pulls the piece from your hand. You pull it out; then in it goes again, and her hair tumbles over her face as she rolls her head and hips in frenetic motion.

Coitus

One final thrust, and you know by the expression on her face that she's reached her orgasm. Now it's your turn.

She's used to being the aggressive one, the boss in the office. Domineering women are often excited by having the tables turned on them in a sexual situation. In your most authoritative manner, tell her that she's had her fun and now it's time for her to pleasure you. Tell her you expect your women to be obedient. Tell her you have ways to handle recalcitrant little girls, but at the same time caress her gently (you don't want to really frighten her). Capricorn is a very clever lady, and she'll know exactly what kind of playacting you have in mind. The idea leaves her shivering with excitement and more than willing to play her role. Order her into the bedroom, and while you seat yourself on the bed, tell her to bring you one of her stockings. Really into her role now, she laughs nervously and hurries to obey you. Order her to kneel in front of you with her back to you. Explain to her that you want her to be completely helpless; then tie her hands behind her back with the stocking, but be certain that you don't hurt her. This little bit of master and slave playacting has given you an erection, and Capricorn just can't wait to see what you have planned for her. Still sitting on the edge of the bed, position the lady between your knees. She should at this point have a pretty good idea of what's coming next. Tell her that she must perform fellatio on you until you reach orgasm, and tell her that her performance better be brilliant or else ... By now you've got her so excited she's practically reached orgasm herself. Down goes her head, and you've never been kissed, nipped, and licked that way before. You want it to last forever, but it's impossible to hold out against Capricorn's willing mouth. While you're getting back your breath, the lady is telling you that she never realized what a strong, masterful man you really were. Tell her you're not through with her yet, which is what she's been dying to hear anyway. With her hands still tied behind her, lift her onto the bed. Now is your opportunity to explore every lovely inch of Miss Capricorn. The more your hands wander and probe, the more excited she'll become. At this point she'll be moaning that she wants more of you. Tell her you don't want to enter her yet. The more you fondle her, the more urgent her pleadings become, and the combination has given you another erection. When she begs you to enter her, pleading that she can't stand it any longer (and to be truthful, you're about to come any moment), enter her and drive your penis into her. Your mutual orgasms will be the sweetest release either of you has ever known. There'll be no doubt in her mind who her master is from now on.

Post-coitus

A no-nonsense shower, quick nap to refresh, she's up and dressed in casual clothes. It's time to have a nice chat about your prospects, who you know, and how well you're connected.

As she's going over your Rolodex of names, you marvel at her flexibility. No less than an hour or two ago you both were locked in the exquisite act of sex. A communion, you thought, of two vibrant people, giving their body and spirit to each other. Hold on, why should you complain? If you're the man that houses all the things she desires, including a one-way ticket to success and money, why not do it with this sensational woman?

You can bet your life that at the next cocktail party she gives, you'll be co-host, meeting all the right people and finding all the proper contacts. You're on your way up the ladder; she's on your side and prodding you from one rung below.

AQUARIUS
(January 21–February 19)

The Aquarius Man

Recognition

The Aquarius male is exciting, dynamic, brilliant, eccentric, confusing, and a thoroughly strange sign of the zodiac. When we realize that over seventy percent of personages in the Hall of Fame were born under this sign or have Aquarius ascending, it's apparent that truth is the essence of this man's life. Still, there's a naïveté and directness about him, and he's constantly and forever endeavoring to avoid marriage if he possibly can.

Mankind is his interest, more so than isolated men or women, and where his family, his blood relatives, are concerned, he's very involved. The Aquarian is usually physically attractive, medium tall, strong, and well-built, with a habit of holding his handsome head to one side while he listens or answers questions or talks himself. His features are regular, with few curves. The face is composed of straight, angular planes, as is his body. His eyes are usually neither large nor small, but extremely alert, penetrating, and personal, and range from pale blue to a purple-brown.

The nose is well-shaped. This man is easily bored by old ideas, and his face will become a flexible and fluent mask of disdain, at other times expressive and funny to watch. His hair may range from light blond to brown, even to black. His good physique will remain as he ages.

He's a blast when it comes to wardrobe, when he's in one of his offbeat moods, affecting a weird display of flower-child fashions, vest open with no shirt, gypsy pants with a scarf instead of a belt. For business, however, he'll be smartly tailored and well-coordinated. His tie, though, will be flamboyant.

His jewelry is kooky, not usually settling around the old school ring. His rings could be two snakes entwined, possibly covering the entire lower part of his finger, or maybe a cameo of Caesar or Napoleon, and on the pinky an ankh sign or an Egyptian scarab. He favors chunky stones, and will often refuse to wear watches, because any constriction around wrist or waist is annoying to him. Besides, he's got an alarm system in his brain and usually knows what time it is.

Good slacks and sports jacket may be offset by wild shoes with colorful platforms. He's a delightful contradiction; cheerful most of the time, but elusive as a feather in a breeze, not generally wanting to be pinned down to a one-to-one relationship. He can love you insanely, but remain as elusive as a handful of sand. If you hold him too tightly, he'll slip through your fingers, but if you just keep your palm upward, the sand stays, and so does the Aquarian male. He won't tolerate the smallest limitations; he wants to be free to think, act, and move.

Along with this offbeat cat goes an under-the-surface patience for mankind and its frequent failure at expressing its ideas and realizing its potential. This love for humanity is combined with a telepathic pickup, enabling him to "send" out his thoughts. Even when things go badly, inner courage and patience are his salvation. For the Aquarian there's always tomorrow, and it'll usually be a far better day than today. He's an "up" personality, so don't try to pin him "down."

While he's with you, you're number one, but ten minutes later he can be off on another tangent. Although his patience for others is supreme, he's highly impatient with himself. To him, the world's got to move, it's got to happen "today," and he's got to help make it happen. If there are frustrating deals, it's at times like these that the Aquarian will display his uncontrollable temper. It can explode like a volcano, not usually at anyone else, but at himself for his inability to control a given situation.

He's realistic, and his sense of humor is as odd as the rest of his characteristics. He enjoys shocking others with his conduct on occasion, often getting on a crazy kick and doing idiotic things like jumping in a pool with all his clothes on. He has the virtue of being friendly to just about everybody, even if he doesn't like them. But he never really gives himself completely—no close-knit, tight bonds for the Aquarian. Everyone was born free and should remain that way. He's usually a way-out liberal in his ideas, opinionated as to how the world, the country, or even individual people should run themselves. He favors change and abhors violence, but he'll rarely reveal those ideas, because "live and let live" is quite definitely his motto.

Of all the signs, the Aquarian requires the most sleep, really needing his eight or so hours. Otherwise, he becomes unmanageable and irritable.

He's opposed to "do-it-yourself" drugs and has a very low tolerance for medication prescribed. The Aquarian will prefer vitamin pills to keep up his strength rather than submit to a physical examination. His feeling is, "I'm well, how can I be sick?"

Absolutely despising a liar or cheat, he wants the facts straight—good or bad. He can tell a white lie or two himself, but it's more a twisting of the truth to protect others, even if he doesn't like them.

The water bearer has a normal interest in food, but it's not the utmost importance in his life. He sometimes takes off on a health-food binge, gobbling up foods that are "good for you," such as yogurt, cheese, and most vegetables. Really, though, he has little time to make a fetish of dining. He's just as happy to walk through his office with a carton of salad and enjoy it as much as he would a gourmet dinner. He likes lemons, oranges, and limes, in fact, most citrus fruits, but mealtime means very little. He'll eat anything that's around, but only when he's hungry. The Aquarian is usually slender, unless, when on one of his mad kicks, he starts eating all the things "bad for you." One compulsive eating jag can gain ten or fifteen pounds for him very quickly. As for drink, give this man champagne; anything that's bubbly is wonderful to him. Desserts are unimportant, but if pressed, he prefers the light and flaky, rather than the heavy or gooey. He loves coffee and will experiment with every known type and preparation at home and in local coffeehouses.

Where to Find Him

Find him? He's all over the map. Being a combination of all the signs, his abilities are quite varied. A great politician (he loves handshaking), because you never really know whether he's with you or not. He can smile and say one thing, next tell his secretary to "cross that guy off our Christmas list."

The social sciences boast many Aquarians. He could be a successful psychologist, because there's a certain talent of drawing out your problems and at the same time a faculty for inspiring trust. The Aquarian can genuinely help and never, ever reveal your secrets.

An innate ability to diagnose makes him an excellent physician. He is wonderful with children, and working with those that have speech, sight, or hearing defects is a satisfying occupation for the Aquarian.

One might say his extrasensory perception as applied to any sort of teaching works wonders. He can excite the imagination of others. The Aquarian can be an excellent college professor, not only discussing the facts, but stimulating his students by theorizing, giving them an opportunity for growth of their own mental faculties.

As for science, he can easily tread through the mundane day-to-day research and make it exciting for himself. Or you could find him as maître d' or a cruise-line entertainment director, dedicating himself to making people comfortable and happy. If he's aiding man's advancement in any field, the Aquarian has found his niche in life.

His hobbies are offbeat, but hobby or vocation, he's a great handicapper at the racetrack. He enjoys watching the crowds and figuring out their minds and motivations, at the same time using his own ESP to figure out the winners. Inveterate gamblers, these Aquarians, and it's their greatest vice.

Primary Move

The approach to the Aquarian male is quite different from the approach to most other men, because you're dealing with someone who doesn't need, desire, or require any possessive relationship outside of his immediate family. No matter that you secretly harbor long-range plans for him, you've got to get your point across by assuring him you're just looking for fun and an evening of excitement. Be careful, though. He can read your thoughts!

Anything odd and stimulating, providing vicarious thrills, will please him. Suggest a horse or dog race. Even trotters are good fare. Here he can enjoy the fever of the chase as well as his favorite pastime, watching the crowd. If he wins, it's even better.

Grab a hot dog along with him, and relish it. That's dinner for both of you! After the last race, when he's happily given you an imaginary rundown on nine-tenths of the people he's observed, the interest is over in that department. Now he can direct his attention to you. With the excitement caused by gambling now finished, the magnificent animals' competition done, and the busy day shortly coming to a close, he can now apply his energies to helping one of the world's worthiest—you!

He's not the fastest to jump at each and every opportunity to play house, so if you win at the races, be satisfied you made even a dent in his armor. Then, after giving your next move some thought for a day or two, come up with a plan to which he must say yes.

Pre-coitus and Coitus

The Aquarius man seems unapproachable, yet is congenial if you do make the first move. He seems removed from all the turmoil of daily business, yet is very much involved. The Aquarian is a quixotic, self-contained master of life.

He's a complete challenge and a difficult case if you're determined to make him your lover. Are you sincere and willing to expose yourself to lack of affection, desultory dinner conversation, and inconsistency of lovemaking? Are you willing to pay the price? If so, your struggle will be amply rewarded, because the Aquarian Chinese puzzle is the most sensational creator of passion in the zodiac. While people tout the Scorpio and Leo men in sexual successes, they pale compared to the water bearer's inflammable masculinity and virility; but unlike the men of those other signs, the Aquarian often fades in and out of your life. Not so much with his physical presence, but his mind. There he is, but there he's not, at least with you. He's off on some phantasmagoric adventure, a place you'll never find. It's worth the gamble, though, anytime.

Achievement, lust for luxury, and experimentation are consummate in his makeup. You'll be as much a program of research as a love object. Not only will you conceive his indulgence in the joy of sharing a night or more, but your reaction to his touch, his tongue, any tactile intercourse, is part of his sense. Watching and playing and watching again. He'll play the devil's advocate just to get a rise out of you, while taking mental notes as to how this annoys you or how that manipulates your reactions. Rarely does he stop playing "games."

Being very flexible, he adjusts to the meanest surroundings and uncomfortable situations in which he finds himself. Preferably, he loves the grandiose life and comfort, so your first maneuver, planned carefully in all detail, would be to invite him to a resort where you can rent a well-furnished private cottage with available room service. At a beach if you live south, or at a lake if the seashore's not possible. Not a rustic place, but one that is elegant, with Continental cuisine, heated swimming pools, and a bar.

Where money's concerned, he's liberal; in fact, it sometimes flows through his fingers too quickly, like the water sign he is. So if the tab is kind of high, you can be fairly sure he'll pick up the check.

Nonchalant is the word that describes him as he arrives an hour and one-half late. But he's cool and doesn't look as though he just traveled fifty-six miles, nor does he apologize for being delayed. It's been a long day, and if you're perky-looking when you answer his knock and have a cold martini with an olive in hand for him, the ice is broken and the weekend should be a blast. Sun-kissed ladies appeal to his aesthetic sense, and those white spaces accentuated by a golden tan really turn him on.

He acts neither sweet nor affectionate on his arrival, just a handsome, appreciative smile of thanks for your healthy good looks, and even more for that martini-filled frosted glass bobbling that little olive.

As if he's known you all his life, he'll hand you his jacket and take the martini with one hand, loosening his tie and opening his collar with the other. Then he'll turn, with not even a "thank you," and walk to the little terrace outside the cottage to enjoy the lovely view of shimmering water catching the last rays of the afternoon sun. A deep sigh, a long sip, and "Let's go for a swim." He's talking to you, girl, so because you anticipated the swim, you're ready.

He seems to know where the bedroom is, because he lifts

The Lovers' Guide to Sensuous Astrology 169

his overnight case and heads for it like a radar signal was turned on.

In two minutes flat he's back. Glass emptied and handed to you for a refill, he's something else to see in his swimming trunks. A body that spells man-sex-delight!

Downing his second martini with relish and wiping his mouth on his arm, he takes your hand, and you're off and running to his empire—the entire sea. It's all his, and you may join him. Aquarians are usually excellent swimmers, and approaching the shore, he does a ten-yard dash and dives underwater, popping up forty feet away while you wonder if your consort is lost in Davey Jones's locker.

Turning now and swimming with long and even strokes, he surface-dives again and swims underwater until he reaches your bikini bottoms, pulls them off, coming up with them in one hand. That smile again. It's melting! The ocean and its undertow are within you as he grabs your legs to put around his hips and places the bikini bottom on his upper arm like a banner of victory.

There's no prelude to sex with the Aquarian. He finds your bare bottom, and again, like an installed radar device implanted in his fingertips, he knows exactly where to place his erect penis. As he enters your vagina, it's as if all the glow, excitement, and glamour of the seven seas are now one in you. Coitus underwater is a devilishly wonderful thing. While being held in nature's capricious arms, her sea, you're feeling the life of her most ambitious project, the Aquarian man, within you.

Fluid hips, fluid legs, flowing arms. Movement like a camera in slow motion. Just like a movie scene you never want to end. Then he floats, penis still erect and poking its head above the choppiness of the ocean. "Climb aboard," he says, and you do. You land astride him right on the mark, treading water with your hands and arms as you both begin to sink beneath the surface. "Hold your nose," he shouts, and down you go, clasped in his arms, one hand on your nose, the other practically choking him around his neck, your body engulfing his miraculous virility. As you break the surface of the water together, the dream ends in a shower of emerald-green crystals trickling over your eyelids and down your faces as you hear him moan his climax.

"Can you swim? Are you all right?" Aquarian asks. "All right! Wow!" you say. Then nothing more from him. No fumbling caresses, no sweet endearing words, just, "I'll beat you to the shore," he shouts over the sound of the ocean's roar.

You'll secretly think, "Bastard," but say, "Bet I win!" That's doubtful with an Aquarian.

Where pre-coitus ends and coitus begins is a fine line. It's really all one. From the moment he knocked on the door of your cottage, he was "in bed" with you, and that's the thing about him that's devastating. Even if he ignores you, he's infiltrating you—with his smile, his charm, his nonchalance.

Of course, he wins. There he is on the beach, waving your bikini bottoms and laughing because how in the world are you going to leave the sea pantsless? Teasing, he waves goodbye and starts walking to the cottage, shaking with laughter. Fool him, come right out on the beach bare-assed! But before you get a chance to do so, he's made an about-face, dived, and he's back beside you underwater, slipping your feet into your bikini and pulling it up over your bottom. "Race you to the cottage," he challenges. Oh, he's full of fun, like a schoolboy. You make a mad dash, reach the cottage breathless, turn around, and see him slowly strolling toward you, making signs of victory for you and shouting out. "Hurray, the winner!" You think, "Bastard, but such a love, and that smile."

"C'mere," and he smiles. You're undone as well as your bathing suit as you find yourself being led to the bedroom for more of your Aquarian's antics. Amidst varied and sundry bits and pieces of conversation, he reminds you that this is the month of July and you've still not given him his February birthday present. Assuming a long face and a hurt expression, the Aquarian thespian tells you that not remembering him was unforgivable. For a moment, he's got you by surprise. Then you realize he's the biggest put-on of all. Use your own imagination and play his Aquarian games. Tell him you do have a gift (you didn't even know him in February), and you'll be right back.

Rummage through the few things you brought for the weekend. There are those three colorful scarves you brought to match each of your bikinis. Knot them together and tie them under your breasts in a big bow. On a piece of hotel stationery write "Happy Birthday" and pin it on the bow. Scamper back to the bedroom, strike a pose, and present him with your gift. He'll break up, and you can score the first one for you.

Here's one belated birthday present he won't return; in fact, he'll put it to good use immediately. Taking each end of the colorful bow, he'll pull you toward him on the bed and proceed to scatter kisses across your abdomen. Then he'll roll you over across his lap and stroke your buttocks suggestively. Each swipe of the hand brings new and shattering thrills. Weary now of his own games (but you're not), he'll address himself to soundly fornicating, displaying an amazing repertoire of positions and a highly developed potency that keeps his penis in aggressive action for longer than you've ever known in all your vivid experience.

Post-coitus

The playful antics done, games exhausted, he's lost interest. He leaves the bed, not a word spoken, headed for the john. You hear the shower adjusted and then listen to him whistling the French national anthem!

Sort of enjoying the "aloneness," you close your eyes and snuggle down, thinking about how cozy it'll be after his shower. You can lie in his arms and get to know more about each other, so you wait patiently. Then you wait not so patiently. Then you're impatient. Now you're hurt. Now you're angry. "The bastard, where is he?"

Catapulting out of bed, you land in the bathroom. No Aquarian! There he is, out on the terrace in his birthday suit, engrossed in a book, with a drink by his side.

He looks up with a "who-are-you?" expression, then smiles—and your mad is gone.

"Hey, have you got something to eat?" he mumbles.

"The bastard."

The Aquarius Woman

Recognition

Usually slender and of average height, the Aquarius girl is attractive, and to some eyes, haunting and mysterious. She is all this and also a very zany character, changeable and fun. Her complexion is clear, and she ages gracefully. Always with a youthful zip, a dynamic "let's go," there's an "always-tomorrow" attitude about her. This happiness shows in her square, high-cheekboned face and in her eyes, either deep-set or round and filled with intelligence and curiosity. Very rarely do Aquarius women have round faces, tending to the angular jawbone, chin, and cheek. Her nose is attractive and suits her face.

Well-developed breasts and excellent posture announce self-pride and a dignified mien, no matter what's occurring around her.

She wears her hair as she pleases, not according to the popular trend. Her strawberry-blond to auburn to brown hair will be halfway down her back if the style is short, or it'll be curly if the style is straight. She's a bit crazy about her hair, inclined to chop it all off one day and then cry bitterly for two minutes over her loss. The squall over, she's all sunshine again. After all, "It'll grow."

Her personality is like quicksilver, and quite eccentric. When angered, it's not a quick explosion, but lingers a long time. She remembers everything, and is difficult to appease. She'll turn completely off someone after just a couple of spats and walk away from the relationship as if it never existed.

The Aquarian likes new things, and although she's patient with important things, she's bored with long conversations.

She can be a lover one day, an absolute bitch the next. Perseverance is a major asset, sticking to a project until, in some instances, her good judgment tells her there's no solution, and she'll retreat like a good general and admit failure. She's sensitive enough to cry at the world's injustices, and cannot bear to witness individual suffering.

An Aquarius female is preoccupied with the future, with what's next on the world's agenda. Her ability to concentrate qualifies her as an expert in mind over matter. TV, radio, or a brass band cannot distract her from her point of interest.

Where love is concerned, she's extremely independent, highly self-controlled, and finds it somewhat difficult to express warmth and affection. She'll go out of the way to prove her love, but not in a gushy fashion. She feels so deeply that she fears rejection or being used. As a friend or as a lover, she's more faithful than any other sign.

Money is of no great importance, except to provide security and a safe future. No minks or mansions for this girl. She's more interested in the accomplishment of self, of using her mind to its utmost ability and pushing and stretching her imagination and ideas to the fullest. If you're looking for constant passion, don't bother with this girl, for she's not overly physical.

She needs freedom, this Aquarius lady. Don't try to tie her to home or the bedroom, because she's likely to prefer her career over all. As far as fashion goes, she'll affect the latest in clothes, shoes, makeup, and hats, but again she goes against the style tide, wearing minis when everyone else is in maxis. She'll whip up a hat out of a feather boa, and it'll look stunning. She'll wear capes with flair, long skirts, loads of expensive beads and chains, rings, and earrings. The eyeglasses will be in the most daring frames. She won't turn up at the country club or marina in whites. Rather, she'll be in dungarees and sweat shirts, ready to work and exercise her mechanical mind. Her perfumes will be heavy, musky, and of a Far Eastern source. Or, conversely, they'll be fresh, light, and tangy. No in-between for her, no Nuit de Noël or something described as "smelling nice." Her soaps are practical and functional. In fact, she prefers the functional in everything from fountain pens to furniture.

If you're a gourmet, you'll never understand her, because of all the signs, to her food is the least significant factor. She eats to live and would rather take a complete dinner in a pill accompanied with a bubbly champagne. Food tastes are not sensual and heavy foods depress her, bog her down, and halt her thinking. And she's got to be in control. You can bet she'll have pets around, because she dotes on animals, enjoying the free spirit essence of a dog or cat. She has love in her heart, but her freedom of soul restricts her expression of her innermost feelings.

Where to Find Her

Look for her anywhere, everywhere. The Aquarius woman can fit her unusual personality into any business. Her ethics are high, and with constant application she will always do well in her chosen field. She'd make a fine judge or lawyer. Her love of animals may be directed to the research of animal communication or the survival of endangered species. She'd be a fantastic politician, executive, artist, actress, or writer. Totally self-motivated, the Aquarian cannot be bullied or driven. If she doesn't wish to do something, it won't be done. If the approach is good and viable, though, she'll consider it. You'll find her as a stewardess, a navigator, even a pilot. Far Eastern philosophic spiritualism intrigues her, as does yoga. She's liberal in her thinking, vain, hard to understand, and just plain fascinating.

Primary Move

The quite obvious approach to the Aquarius lady has to be through her mind. At first, that is. Then, after she accepts you and experiences a deep stirring of her senses, drop the mental approach and relax her by suggesting a cocktail or two. Invite her to your apartment and send a cab to pick her up—she'll appreciate your thoughtfulness. After a drink or two, be loquacious about what you enjoy, about the artists you like, and discuss the latest avant-garde exhibition. She's a listener, ready to learn, and interested in what you have to say.

How you dress is unimportant; she's more interested in your mind. If you can discuss interesting subjects knowledgeably, she'll be tuned in. Be affectionate and show an interest in her concerns. These are traits she will admire, because she finds this sort of thing so difficult herself. After a trip through an art gallery with detailed, ongoing conversation from you as to style, technique, etc., she'll more than likely be convinced you're fascinating. Take her to a gypsy restaurant with strolling violins, order her a dry, bubbly wine, and if you've hit home, she'll let you know it. Dinner over, eyes alight, she'll be ready for a nightcap, either kind, and will graciously invite you to her place for brandy or liqueur.

Pre-coitus

It's as simple as, "Whose place, yours or mine?" Your primary move was the clincher. Obviously, you did appeal to her mind. Oiled her mental wheels, so to speak. She made her decision a few hours ago. Gypsy violins and wine helped, but, sir, it was already decided.

"Get 'em while they're hot." You've heard that often at the beach or at the ball park. Hot dogs are best when they're hot, and she is too. So it's now. No preliminaries.

She likes the sequestered feeling of a closed room and locked door. It appeals to her sense of the mystic. Removed from the tumult of daily living and sharing her mind and body with you, she wants no interruptions from the outside world.

Her ability to concentrate is so developed, you can be sure you're in for the thrill of a lifetime if you are the object of that concentration.

Fanny Hill, the classic of pornographic literature, is a constant source of stimulation to her. She'll lead you directly to the bedroom, close and lock the door, point to a chair on which to place your clothes, and proceed to undress with no modesty, hanging up her dress and putting away her shoes, just as if you weren't there.

So far, all you've done is be yourself. You're winning, so stay ahead by playing no tricks, no fancy flourishes, just reality.

Bed is like a private garden shared with only one (at least only one at a time). Out comes the book from her bedside stand, and she hands it to you to read certain marked passages. She'll throw a well-shaped leg across yours. No complimentary diversion is necessary. Just say it as it is. As you proceed to read the glowing love scene, it gets more difficult keeping the book steady while she is crawling up your body. Fanny's having cunnilingus with the groundskeeper, and your Aquarian wants some of the same.

Basically of an independent nature and wanting nothing for nothing, she'll articulate her wishes, gulping breaths of air while swallowing your penis. Talking with a finger or food in the mouth is one thing, but with a penis? Remember, she is a little kooky.

She'll talk passionately—but to herself, as if you weren't even present. Annoyed at first that you're being ignored, you'll catch on quickly to her mad method as the book slips out of your hand. Then you'll be amazed at how all her conversation is thrilling you to an ejaculation! Having made you come, she's satisfied. Then she'll slide up between your legs, anxious to tongue-bathe you, flicking her tongue over your belly and chest. Your Aquarian might then reach for your nipples, rolling them between her fingers and tickling you in delightful places. As quickly as she started, she'll stop.

Yes, now she wants a photocopy of her performance by you. Fanny's pants were deliciously damp when she left the forest, and your Aquarius lady is lusting for the same treatment.

Start at her thighs and lick the moist flesh until you reach her pulsing puss. Nuzzle her soft curly patch and then blow your moist breath into her vagina. Dip your fingers in her pussy and watch her squirm with delight. Seeing how successfully this finger business works, continue and elaborate on your efforts. She loves having you rub her clitoris and will let you know it by the passionate sounds she makes. Love play like this produces almost more orgasms with an Aquarian than using your real McCoy. . . . Almost.

Coitus

Turn her on the bed so she's bending over the edge, head down, supporting her torso by keeping her hands flat on the floor at a forty-five-degree angle to the bed. Kneel between her legs, lifting her hips up to target position.

Part the lips of her vagina, exposing the secret place you're about to invade. Tell her what you're going to do. Remember, it's not just the tactile sense, it's the mind you're dealing with. Point your penis into her waiting vagina. Let it spread of its own volition as you force-feed that gaping pink place. More of that fine flower as the penis penetrates. The angle in which you've placed her gives you enough room to enter her up to your scrotum.

Now, pull her body up on the bed, penis in place, holding her hips so you won't slip out. Advise her of your present progress. You'll feel the muscles of her vaginal canal go into spasm as they embrace your erection.

Pull him out and infiltrate again. She's moving vociferously now, verbally begging for more. Pull him out and wedge him in again. She's crying tears of passion. Pull him out and invade again. This time her whimpering is a piercing scream as your penis, hard as wood, explodes effusively within.

She wriggles gratefully to a pillow. Panting, eyes closed, knowing all's well, yet unaware it's done. Lost for long moments in the remembering of the bizarre and sensational skirmish with your superweapon, she has won and lost simultaneously.

If your passion's ebbed, renew your spirit by licking her wounds. Make a comfortable spot for your head close between her out-flung legs. As she lies there on her stomach, place your hand under her pussy, cupping her in your hand. Lick her wounds with compassionate concern. You'll feel the muscles within her vagina contract again, releasing the last of her honeysuckle juices.

Post-coitus

Sexually exhausted, she sleeps. Tuck her in, covering her bare shoulders and caressing her neck. She'll sleep until noon tomorrow.

You've excited her mind and body, and now that it's morning, she wants to know everything about you. She'll ask how you brush your teeth, and who cuts your hair, and where do you buy your clothes, and what do you want for breakfast?

Soon your nostrils will be greeted by odors of fresh coffee brewing and bacon frying. You'll learn soon enough that a day without an Aquarian is a day without sunshine.

PISCES (February 20–March 20)

The Pisces Man

Recognition

That guy you see hurrying along, with a well-built torso, is your Pisces male. He's of average height and has small hands, but he's proud of them. They're well-manicured (but no polish, please) and are used with care and emphasis while he speaks. They're not feminine or pudgy, but very deft and graceful. His disposition and opinions are quite often strongly affected by those around him, and his hands make points whether he's dead against or totally and happily for something.

The Pisces male tends to have a full face, often appearing with a charming smile. He should watch his diet, because he could easily put on a few unwanted pounds. The eyes are full, never small or beady, very aware, with extreme perception in his glance. His highly intuitive, overly sensitive nature is readily reflected in his eyes, usually hazel to brown, and one can tell immediately how the Pisces male reacts. His eyes are a giveaway. He's usually not good at stud poker or five-card draw. He wears no mask.

The Piscean has a wide mouth and a wonderful smile, open and friendly. When warm and loving, he's the most fantastically, overtly amorous partner one could wish, and highly sensual in his observations. Anything curvaceous or roundly symmetrical, not just female, stirs him. He's exceedingly vir-

The Lovers' Guide to Sensuous Astrology 179

le, and most Pisceans are blessed with a full head of hair, dark brown to black.

The Pisces man is moody in the extreme, and carries himself according to his mood. If he wakes up to a pleasant morning, having slept well, and has a fine breakfast, he's happy and walks with a brisk step. But once in the office, if something happens to turn him off, his gait changes immediately. Unnerved within, he shows it in his carriage. Pisceans are not easy to understand unless you've been around them for a while. But if you observe their physical manifestations, you can pretty well gauge their moods.

He's idealistic, the Piscean, with an urge to do good and to accomplish a job in a detailed, orderly manner. He's a keen observer of deficiencies in others, but hesitant about commenting on these faults. He's excellent in a personnel situation, with almost telepathic insight, seemingly able to read your thoughts.

The Pisces guy will appreciate any thoughtfulness on your part, because he naturally loves attention and affection. He's very emotional and absolutely delightful to be around. Strangely inconsistent is a frequent lack of self-confidence, since he's versatile, quick to understand, and doesn't deserve this self-inflicted hurt.

Secretive in their innermost being, Pisceans express themselves fully only when involved in passion and love, areas highly important to them.

When low, the Pisces male wants only to withdraw from society and get away by himself, usually by the water, to work out his problems and revitalize his energies.

Pisces isn't at all concerned about what he wears. Not that he doesn't have good taste, he just isn't interested in clothes. It's best to let someone else do his shopping. His agreeable nature and trusting self allow him to rely on just any salesman's advice. It's fortunate that clothes are not a big item with this man, because shopping alone results in a "Salvation Army" look.

He enjoys the deep fire of the amethyst stone because it turns on his mysterious feel for Eastern imagery.

Scents should be spicy and of the sea, fresh, crisp, and bracing. For women, the mystic scents are preferred, the sort that linger long after the lady's left his presence. He loves deep colors, like royal purples, rich blues, and crimson reds. Although he may infrequently wear these shades, he enjoys seeing them on others. The most attractive color is not a color at all, but white, sheer glistening white, pure like rain or snow. When he stays with this passion for white, there can't be too many fashion mistakes. In this area he knows his liabilities and prefers to play it safe.

He loves funny practical jokes, especially those put over with a perfectly straight face, but not the kind of practical jokes that hurt or embarrass others.

Where to Find Him

Representing the twelfth sign of the zodiac, the Pisces male is a composite of every one of the other signs. He might very well be your own personal accountant handling all your tax returns or involved in a charitable organization's finances, or the head of the fund-raising department of a large university. He may contribute his time to causes if he feels they're of great worth. Career-wise, he's usually one of the highest paid in his field, because he's extremely capable.

Here is a marvelous airplane mechanic, because he loves the mystery of flying as well as the myriad technical details. Check all the different courses in school, because he's a born teacher, as well as an avid student. Many Pisceans will be found in the political arena, but in the appointive rather than the elective scheme of things. The fierce competition and muckraking when running for office are abhorrent to them. Like the Librans, their judgment is excellent, and with their innate highly developed perception they make fine judges. Pisces men also make great bartenders because of their empathy to the problems of others, listening to customers' stories as if they were the most important matters in the world.

The Pisces man enjoys golf, tennis, water-skiing, basketball, and baseball. In fact, almost any sport except the excessively violent ones. Wrestling he sees as being phony, and boxing is bloody. You rarely will find him at stock-car races, either. He avoids an atmosphere that suggests or often results in danger, destruction, and death. He's drawn to sports for fun and likes the ones where people don't usually get hurt.

You may find him in a creative-writing course or teaching one. Or even pottery making, where he's very attracted to the sensuous movement of water on clay. Chipping away at marble or granite is in opposition to his nature—too noisy, troublesome, and dusty.

Primary Move

The Pisces man would probably go fishing every Sunday if he could, so suggest an afternoon date on the water and emphasize friendship as opposed to romance at first. He's a very adept fisherman, whether out at sea or along the reefs, enjoying all aspects of preparation, baiting, helping the captain run the boat, putting up the flags, or steering the course.

Wear white, and you'll wow him. Clean, glistening white really appeals to the Pisces male. Wear a man-tailored short-sleeved shirt partially buttoned, breasts not totally in view but at least available. Short shorts, clean white sneakers, a white bandana in your hair—this will suit him, capturing his eye in appreciation of you. The combination of white and your best suntan will turn him on. You can come on strong by just talking and being sweet, friendly, warm, and concerned.

Flatter his ability as a fisherman, and you can bet he'll catch more fish than anyone else on the jaunt.

He'll be sensitive to how you cast, too. If you're ready to make him your partner, keep your vision high and your conversation on a cheerful level. Make him laugh, and laugh right back at his jokes, corny or not.

It's been a long day, and since you're no doubt loaded down with a hearty catch of fish, there's nothing better than extending an invitation for a fish fry at your place.

Since fresh fish is truly his favorite food, the preparation of the fish for cooking should be simple and easy for him. After the fish are cleaned, be the perfect hostess and either barbecue, broil, or fry it.

Cuisine-wise, the Piscean possesses subtle tastes, but he consumes a great deal, so cook plenty. Delicate, exotic seafood; unique, strange fish; and all manner of shellfish, escargots, bouillabaisse, oyster stew, clam chowder, and scallops satisfy the inner Piscean man. He's excellent at preparing a fine dinner, but he approaches it as he would the finalizing of a tax form. And he leaves a terrible mess, having pressed into service every available pot and pan in the kitchen. So make sure you do the culinary honors. He prefers steamed vegetables for their vitamin content, and hates anything overcooked. If he is served something overdone in a restaurant, more often than not he won't make a scene. It's not his nature to hassle the waiter, but he won't eat the food and probably won't dine there again. Pre-dinner, he likes raw vegetables and olives, for both the taste and color involved. Capers and herbs like basil and oregano also please him. Serve him a vinaigrette dressing on his salad, with anchovies. Anything with a salty, fishy, spicy flavor, and you ring a bell. For dessert he'll head for the most sumptuous available, all rich puddings, raspberry turnovers, or chocolate sauce with almonds and whipped cream over pound cake!

As to alcohol, something like one dry martini (with at least three olives) will suffice, two at the very most. The Piscean doesn't need much in the way of alcohol to turn him toward happy conversation. He has a faculty for developing interesting discussions at the dinner table, and is at his best when smiling, chatting, communicating. It's then his digestion is good and all's right with his particular world.

Dinner is a great way to develop a warm relationship with him and to let him know you're very much aware of his many fine accomplishments. At the same time, in a subtle way lead the conversation to his view about love and romance.

Wander in front of him aimlessly, with a puzzled expression, seeming undecided on how to approach him.

He'll easily see what's troubling you. His ESP factor is high, and to save you the embarrassment of appearing overly aggressive, you will be invited to stop pacing and join him at the piano, where he's been entertaining you.

When you're sitting thigh-to-thigh on the bench, he'll bend across you to reach for some music, brushing deliberately across your breasts. The intended stimulus is quite clear. He's being obvious in order to present you with an easy opportunity.

When he has the gift of psychic awareness, as particular signs of the zodiac do, he often uses it to ease the progress of any situation. The Piscean male is not only tuned in to your sexual drive for him, but wants you to experience the thrill of cornering your prey—him. He's given you your cue, so go to it. Slip your arms around his neck, pressing your body close to his. Your warm body, a degree over normal temperature, will speak for you. Unbutton his shirt and nuzzle your face in his hairy chest. Tease the hairs gently with your teeth, starting at his breastbone and working your mouth to his nipples. Continue to caress his chest with your lips, sucking his nipples each time you pass by. He's a very sensitive fellow, and although his reaction won't bring a climax, his nipples and penis will both become erect.

The Lovers' Guide to Sensuous Astrology 183

Pisces man's perceptiveness is bearing fruit. He knew if he gave you half a helping hand at the start, you'd end up capturing him sexually. You need no more urging to continue.

Pre-coitus

You have to be limber and somewhat of an acrobat to slip to your knees from the piano bench while you're unzipping his trousers. He'll help though; he loves the idea of what you're going to do next, and again his mystic senses tell him what to do to cooperate. The Pisces man will rise to make it easier for you to finish what you started. Offer his protruding penis a kiss and a promise while excusing yourself to change.

While you're slipping into a pure white, totally misleading, virginal-looking negligee and spraying yourself with a sexy-scented perfume, he has a chance to step out of his slacks and shorts, recline on the sofa, and wait for you.

If upon your return you find some of the iron gone out of his erection, just slip it between you lips and suck. Take it out of your mouth with your hand and examine your handiwork, then back in your mouth again, drawing it up and up. It won't be long before Pisces has another fantastic hard-on.

Fellatio is a divine activity for the Pisces male. He's of such an emotional nature that your tongue expertise could produce an immediate space shot. Watch his penis spurt, see how far the semen shoots. Your Piscean will get an extra thrill watching you watch the action.

In moments like this, when two are just starting their journey into sex, it's necessary to work from a clean slate, so to speak. There are several ways to clean up the residue. If you're really into sex and feel very deeply emotionally about lovemaking with him, lick it off his belly with your tongue, disposing of it into a towel. If you can't make that scene, which by the way would immediately give him another erection, use a washcloth and wipe it away.

In any event, comfort is now the order of the moment. Help remove the balance of his clothing. As you stand together, let him unbutton your robe, dropping it to the floor in order to display your eager body.

The Piscean tends to a hairy body, which is most wildly exciting as he holds you close in his arms. Some of the two-fish sign shave their chests. If he does, don't be surprised. Rubbing your breasts against prickly hairs is better than it sounds. It's a devastating, sensuous experience, so enjoy it.

He found pleasure in your ministrations and wants to reciprocate. Do a "Helen Morgan" thing and sit on the top of the baby grand. Standing in the curve of the piano, he can achieve direct contact with your excited clitoris. Tonguing gently at first, then probing more and more insistently into your vagina makes for your climactic moment. Pisces' penis, once again swollen, is ready for the next number on the program.

Coitus

Lead him down the primrose path to white sheets scented with perfume and bowls of gardenias near the bed.

Lying on the bed smelling of sweet and fragrant flowers, Pisces will feel splendidly attentive to your next move. But you're not ready to have him make the plunge. Time to use your head (and hands)! The Pisces man will love your inventiveness. Your searching for the hidden secrets of his body invites incredible ardor. Tell him about the Oriental trick that will titillate unbelievably, the Silk Cord Caper. He's amenable to anything.

Using props with a Pisces male is fun in sex and not unusual. So if you're the least inhibited, loosen up and throw away your hang-ups. Part one of the caper requires that you invest in a one-foot-long pure silk cord an eighth of an inch thick. It should be precisely knotted on one end, not too bulbous, just the size of a dried green pea. Now, heavily lubricate the cord. Mineral oil is kind of messy, so try Vaseline. He's ready for anything when first your middle finger is plunged in the same Vaseline jar. Very gently and slowly insert the knotted end into his anus. You've not only got to be an acrobat, but ambidextrous as well. As you push the cord in with one hand, the other hand is lovingly stroking his scrotum. Something like the Chinese torture treatment, but not painful, rather sexually thrilling.

Once the cord is inserted with enough exposed to control with certainty, you are ready for part two of the Silk Cord Caper. Your hand, anointed with petroleum jelly, moves to his penis and vigorously manipulates it. The combined effort of each hand brings fantastic compensation. It's happening now! Upon that moment of ejaculation, pull the cord hard! Your Piscean man will remember this free-fall without a parachute forever. The cord's out, you are in.

This night, history will be written for him. Your Piscean

male will always tingle when remembering your erotic inventions.

He's all nerve ends now, ready to move in answer to your silent but urgent call. Even if he's deaf, he's got to know you're ready by those churning hips.

Let him be the aggressor, or if you wish, tell him how you like coitus. Which position gives you the greatest kick. After all, you were so busy pleasing him you had no time for any action yourself. That is, unless you're strictly a voyeur, and watching his pleasure has already brought you to orgasm.

Post-coitus

After your exhausting experiences, he'll be tired but tender. Hugging, caressing, sweetly kissing your hair and forehead, he'll tell you you're the most fascinating woman he's ever met.

From now on, you'll be awfully busy manufacturing little episodes to please him, but it's worth it if you really want that Pisces male.

The Pisces Woman

Recognition

The Pisces woman is one of the great beauties of the zodiac. Her skin is luminous, shiny like alabaster, most often light-complexioned, tender, and feathery to the touch. She constantly has to be aware of exposure to the sun. Five minutes too long and she'll have lobster-red burns taking weeks to heal. Aware from childhood that particular attention has to be paid to her body as well as her face, she indulges herself in body creams, lotions, and protective under-makeup bases.

From short to middle height, she possesses full, liquid, romantic eyes, and when aroused, a hot and sexy glint appears. Piscean's hair is usually thick and beautiful, tumbling lavishly over her shoulders and manageable in any sort of coiffure. Loose, free-flowing styles that frame her face like a Renoir painting or soft curls falling lightly on her forehead and shoulders are reminiscent of Gainsborough's *Blue Boy*.

She's a lovely little creature, with small hands, generally professionally manicured, and beautifully formed feet, equally well cared for. Shoes are a fetish with the Pisces woman, and she loves to buy exquisitely made sandals to exhibit her painted toes and lovely feet. She buys shoes in the bright colors and the newest look, from four-inch platforms to five-inch Louis XIV heels. Rarely does she make a mistake in being badly shod.

Her taste in clothes could be called adventurous or funky, and everything in regard to the purchase of them is practically ritualized. She'll never just "buy" like most other women. The selection and fitting must be in the nature of a shopping expedition. The Pisces woman often develops in her circle of friends a Leo lady shopping companion with excellent taste who will restrain her from indulging in some of her wilder impulses. Leo females can buy for themselves as well as for others. The Piscean, when properly attired, can emerge looking like what she is—a beautiful doll.

A delicate touch and a whimsical smile characterize the Pisces girl, a lady who finds her own dream world far more desirable and real than reality itself. One of her major problems is confusing fondness and compassion for true love. Perhaps it's her inability to distinguish one from the other that makes her forever ready and willing to substitute any emotional feeling for love. She's very much affected by the men in her life, and can easily be the mirrored reflection of their moods. Normally, she's good-natured and easygoing but extremely impressionable. She'll cry easily at someone's hard-luck story and is quick to offer sympathy—or she'll happily celebrate someone's good luck, vicariously thrilled at their good fortune. You might wonder upon meeting her why the Pisces woman tends to lack self-confidence and self-esteem, since she is so lovely. This factor in the Pisces nature varies in degree from one woman to another, but it is usually present to some extent.

She adores little pets; the Yorkshire terrier, miniature poodle, and Chihuahua are her favorites. You'll find her snuggling and mothering and walking through life with a furry creature in her arms. In fact, small animals of all kinds give her pleasure, and she has a faculty for taming wild squirrels and chipmunks. They'll come right up to her hand to receive a nut, or linger on her windowsill to catch a glimpse of their Pisces lady.

She can grow ecstatic just by looking at a peaceful countryside, a garden of cultivated flowers, or a field of wild ones. She's extremely psychic and senses things before they actually occur. She has a predisposition to precognition. It's not an unusual sight to see her eyes open wide in surprise as she exclaims, "I just knew that was going to happen!" Too bad her psychic awareness doesn't carry through to men. In matters of love, because of her empathy and passionate nature, she can't tell the difference between a guy on the make and a man sincerely interested in her.

Where to Find Her

Her delicate feet serve a multipurpose. Aside from being beautiful and supporting her body, they can sometimes earn her a living. Gifted dancers, these Pisces girls. Light and fast on their feet, they move with a grace and ease that's lovely to watch. The Piscean will be very successful as a professional dancer if she has the ability to stick with the training and discipline required. She makes a great stripper, combining the qualities of a seductive, sexy-looking woman with her natural dancing talent. These attributes could make her a star in this field.

Any creative activity or artistic endeavour attracts her—painting, sculpture, ceramics. She's not for banging away with a chisel and hammer, but best at forming clay with those small but clever hands.

She's able, through intuitive qualities, to express herself magnificently as an actress. She feels the character just by thinking. Guided through the creation of a role with a strong figure on which to rely, she could find less success in the offing in the theater.

She's also content working where no personal decisions are required and where the procedures are prepared and laid out for her, to repeat by rote and carry on to a conclusion. When working in a stock-brokerage house or as an insurance actuarian, if the work is deeply detailed, the Pisces woman can take over and do it.

188 *Marlowe and Urna Gray*

In any position in which her five senses (the psychic sense is number five) can be utilized, she'll find success. You can often locate her as co-owner of a restaurant or hostess or cook in a gourmet operation. Her delight and taste in food are subtle and exotic. Many Pisceans are excellent cooks and knowledgeable gourmets. They enjoy fish of all types, rather delicately prepared. Sucking the lobster meat from the shell is almost a sexual experience for her; ordering a succulent dish for favorite customers is most satisfying, especially when they rave. She knows the special dishes people like to eat.

Serve her olives, or veal dishes with wine or lemon sauce, and she's sure that it's what everyone enjoys, or should. For dessert, a crisp, tasty brown Betty can be as desirable as crêpes suzette. As you see, her tastes are of an elegant yet an unusual sort, just as they are in sex.

Pre-coitus

She's not shy in sex, and she is often a reflection of your mood. If you're horny and playful, she is. How about strip poker? Adolescent and old-fashioned, perhaps, but she loves old things, even games. Using a new deck of cards, direct her to shuffle thoroughly, removing the jokers. Her ability to handle details will be satisfied, and she'll be certain you're not cheating. What you're doing is building trust, and you're also setting a pattern of giving commands for her to follow obediently.

The Pisces lady is always ready to cooperate. The happiest moments of her life are when she's doing something for someone that gives pleasure or assistance. She's so susceptible to being influenced by so-called "vibes" that one must be in good spirits around her. Otherwise, you'll find her demeanor and attitude slipping one notch below your own "down."

Although not of a slavish nature, she loves a man to be domineering and forceful, a man who can guide and direct the moment, take hold of situations and be her rock of Gibraltar. Someone she can cling to and with whom she can find the protection in life she so sorely needs. A man that can satisfy this serious aspect of her nature is amply rewarded by her trust and devotion.

In your version of strip poker, set your own ground rules. Make a switch in the game. Instead of the loser removing clothes, the winner has the honors.

First deal, and Pisces wins. Off come her shoes, but with

The Lovers' Guide to Sensuous Astrology

élan. Second deal, Pisces wins again, and off come her slacks. Your fingers fumble as you unzip her fly, caressing her pussy as you slide the zipper down. "Did I hurt you?" you say. "Let me kiss it and make it better."

Give her a generous, wet kiss right through the nylon panties to the downy-haired triangle as she steps out of her slacks. Win or lose the game, you're a winner!

Third deal, you win. So sad? She removes your double-knit flares; the socks and shoes can wait. It seems that fumbling fingers are contagious, because her hand gets caught on a large sky-hook jutting out of your Jockey shorts. As you know, it's give and take with her. With lusciously opened mouth, she'll nibble your erection right through the white cotton Jockey shorts.

At this point, like a shrewd card player, throw in the deck and admit she wins.

You'll grab for her, but she'll squirm away from you, wiggling her round bottom while unhooking her brassiere. Before she realizes it, you're behind her, slipping your penis between her cheeks, panties pushed aside, aiming for her already moist vagina.

"Why fight fate?" she thinks. She's a true believer in destiny and will bend to it and you, allowing easy entrance from the rear.

Lubricate the tip of your penis with saliva. Homemade products are always better. Gleaming with purpose, insert and cautiously feel your way as she moves her derriere in just the right position to assist you.

This Pisces lady is living her sign to the hilt, and so are you, up to yours. Stay in there; don't withdraw. Use a rocking motion inside like an in-place roller-coaster ride. Then push, up to the very tip of the cervix as the muscles of her vagina contract, milking you to orgasm.

Now, take off your Jockey shorts and her lacy pants.

She's extremely courteous and affable by nature, and inventive enough to come up with new thrills of her own.

The dining-room table covered with a sheet is a wonderful spot for further examination. A long flat table on which to lie, bright lights overhead, and she's got a perfect view of you.

She'll probably ask you to lie lengthwise on the table, so you'll fit on it with just your legs hanging over, bent on the edge of the table at your knees. While you are making the precipitous climb, she'll return to the living room for a pillow to put under your head.

Now, posting herself at the end of the table between your knees, her full breasts swaying with every move, she asks you to take your penis in hand. She wets it with her own saliva to assist your easy hand movement. Now she's set to watch you masturbate. Strange, but why not?

You never dreamed you'd be playing the adolescent to please a passionate Piscean. But you will, and you'll enjoy it as much as she will.

Coitus

She deliberately holds a breast in each hand. Now she is cupping them, handling them, and tickling the nipples as you watch while you are jerking away.

Then she sticks her tongue out at your throbbing penis, moving it up and down, miming the way one eats an ice-cream cone that's melting around the edges.

You say the last time you masturbated you were eleven? Maybe so, but never like this.

When the Piscean sees that you are ready to discharge, she'll crawl upon the table, slide your penis within her lips, and catch your come in her mouth.

Say, who was going to make whom?

After she's watched you masturbate, her vagina is desperately yearning for you to fill it. All that's happened is still not the main event. She'll feel rejected if you don't go further. Everyone enjoys a change, so off you amble to the bedroom. So far, you've cavorted in every room in the apartment, a total three-room circus.

She knows what she wants, and won't hesitate to ask you to sit on the side of the bed. The Pisces woman will then face you, climb on your lap, and then spread her legs so she can wrap them around your hips. In this position, a springy bed can help.

Pisces is now unbearably excited, and there's no controlling her, so don't even try. She's wildly rotating her hips, grinding your penis deeper and deeper into her vagina and then bouncing up again with the help of the bed springs. Meanwhile you're sucking her breasts until you can tell by the change in her breathing that she is about to come. Just as she reaches orgasm, you ejaculate deep inside her.

Post-coitus

This Pisces lady, hot hips and all, may want to lie on top of you for a while. It's never really over for her if you're up to it. So be gentle if you're through. Slide her beside you; she will slither, because her body's wet with love. Run your fingers across her brow and through her hair to calm her down.

As mentioned before, she'll do just as you desire, and in a moment or two you'll have your tigress-turned-kitten sleeping soundly in the crook of your arm. You really have it made when it's a Piscean you're after.

ASTROLOGY...FOR YOU!

Your Own Personal Computerized Horoscope reveals...

- **What You Are All About**
- **Your Life Style**
- **Your Success Potential**
- **Your Future... Next 12-Months Forecast!**

The wisdom of Astrology has enlightened people all over the world for over 5,000 years. And... now more than ever. You can share in this knowledge through your own personal computerized horoscope. It tells you more about yourself.

10 Full Pages All About You

SPECIAL OFFER... $8.00 VALUE FOR ONLY $4.00

HOROSCOPE ORDER BLANK (PLEASE PRINT CLEARLY)
INCLUDE $4.00 CHECK OR MONEY ORDER MADE OUT TO: THE NEW AMERICAN LIBRARY

SEND TO: HOROSCOPE OFFER
THE NEW AMERICAN LIBRARY, INC.
P.O. BOX 999, BERGENFIELD, NEW JERSEY 07621

Name_____

Address_____

City_____ State_____ Zip_____

My Date of Birth: Month_____ Day_____ Year_____

My Time of Birth: _____ A.M. / P.M. (circle one)
(If time is unknown, 12 noon will be used)

My Place of Birth: (check one)
- ☐ Eastern Time Zone
- ☐ Pacific Time Zone
- ☐ Central Time Zone
- ☐ Foreign Country _____
- ☐ Rocky Mt. Time Zone

Allow 6 weeks for delivery of horoscope. Offer void where prohibited by law. The decision to believe or reject the report is that of the recipient.